40 DAYS WITH GOD IN THE GARDEN

HEALING HEARTS WITH GARDEN GRACE

40 DAYS WITH GOD IN THE GARDEN

HEALING HEARTS WITH GARDEN GRACE

MELODY LOWES

authorHOUSE®

AuthorHouse™
1663 Liberty Drive
Bloomington, IN 47403
www.authorhouse.com
Phone: 1-800-839-8640

Published by AuthorHouse   06/15/2012

ISBN: 978-1-4772-0897-7 (sc)
ISBN: 978-1-4772-0898-4 (hc)
ISBN: 978-1-4772-0899-1 (e)

Library of Congress Control Number: 2012909081

Contents

DEDICATION

To Jesus, who has taught me to see Him as He is, as I linger in my garden.
To my husband Brent, who has loved me so well through life's most difficult seasons.

SPECIAL THANKS

To Rosemary Foley (editor):
your insights and input has been invaluable.
Thank you!

INTRODUCTION
In The Beginning . . .

*"For everything there is a season, a time
for every activity under heaven."*
Ecclesiastes 3:1

Ah, the garden.

A place of beauty and refreshment. A place of work rewarded, joy and frustration, laughter and growth. A place of healing and determination, peace and reflection.

All life was seeded, embryonic with promise, beneath Eden's verdant boughs. In the beginning, God tucked the first of us into a garden He himself designed. Everything beautiful and fresh and delightful sprang up from that perfect soil.

Ironically, the roots of all of life's struggles and turmoil also sprang from that Edenic ground—in the guise of a tempting fruit, which captured the imagination of the human race. It is therefore perfectly possible that the ingredients necessary for healing our deepest wounds can be discovered here, where it all began, within the garden gate.

So enter through the arch. Stroll the paths. Smell and see and ponder.

The botanical world has much to teach us about life and death, harvest and hope. It portrays the human experience in miniature, in leafy parallel. The garden is hallowed ground where life lessons are acted out in seasonal regularity—and it will impart its wisdom if we are wise enough to seize it with willing hearts and hands.

Come with me to the garden. Let me draw your eye to some of the green and healing truths that I have encountered there. Consider these simple stories a fruitful harvest, ripe for the picking—a rich soul-food to nourish your hurting heart on its long and tedious journey.

May the roots of your soul dig deeper, the vines of your dreams reach higher, the blooms of your heart unwind in more glorious triumph for having been in the garden, where God-whispers have echoed through every season from the beginning . . .

SPRING

"A time to plant . . ."
—Ecclesiastes 3:2

"My mind is a garden. My thoughts are the seeds.
My harvest will be either flowers or weeds."
—Mel Weldon

Love Planted A Garden

You need to know something about me up-front.

I get almost rabid to plant something—anything—by the time spring arrives.

I absolutely love planting things. Seeds. Scrappy little bedding plants, brimming with bloom. Perennials. Bulbs, brittle and bland. Grass. Trees.

Any sprig of green that might make my world more beautiful gets its turn with my spade and trowel. And I have noticed that this desire for yard beautification, park perfection, and space-sprucing, doesn't begin or end with me.

It seems that most of us have a drive toward either enjoying visually pleasing places, or creating them—or both.

Why?

The truth is, the appreciation of beauty began millennia ago, in the heart of our Master Gardener Himself. And since we are created in

God's image, we have inherited His singular drive to create beautiful living spaces.

God's first action after creating the universe—galaxies and gravity, peacocks and pansies, hyenas and humans—reveals much about His character. He didn't jump over Jupiter, or do dot-to-dots with the stars. He didn't ride a rainbow or muck about with tectonic plates for a laugh.

Of all the things He could have done, He got out His gardening gloves!

"Then the Lord God planted a garden . . ."
(Genesis 2:8)

The author of Genesis goes on, **"The Lord God made all sorts of trees grow up from the ground—trees that were beautiful and that produced delicious fruit." (Genesis 2:9)**

Why would it matter to Him that the trees were 'beautiful'? Or that what they produced was 'delicious'? Why would He have designed such an intricately balanced plant world, one that would feed us, medicate us, oxygenate us, and provide us with building supplies, textiles, and art materials?

It's a fascinating peek into the way God thinks. Into His motivations. Into the vast purposes generated by that intensely creative brain. Into His heart desires for those He created.

He's **crazy** about us!

Loving all things lovely, He made human beings, faded and lesser but accurate copies of His soul, and planted us in the loveliest place His rich imagination could conceive.

A garden . . .

A garden is a symbol of hope—no war-time people in the throes of survival take the time to plant. There is too much likelihood of never reaping the benefits! No, gardens are a distinctly peaceful and prosperous feature of forward thinking, an investment in the future that is delicious and nourishing to body and soul alike. No wonder we like to spend time there.

*"**When the cool evening breezes were
blowing, the man and his wife heard the
Lord God walking about in the garden.**"
(Genesis 3:8)*

Some things haven't changed much since God walked about in Eden. Take a look in your local park in the cool of the evening, and you will find many who enjoy the beauty and stillness of outdoor spaces in much the same way as our Maker. Relaxing, barefoot toes in sod, noses teased by seasonal scents, we take to the open air to redeem the day.

Loving us so well, the Master Gardener has given us tools for reproducing shades of Eden. Hiding within our hearts is an implanted craving for some of the things He values—beauty, fresh air, lush growth, soft grass, flowering shrubs, fruit trees. It gives Him pleasure to share these good gifts, to give *us* pleasure.

Maybe that is why He has a garden planted in heaven itself.

*"**. . . On each side of the river grew a tree of life, bearing
12 crops of fruit, with a fresh crop each month. The
leaves were used for medicine to heal the nations.**"
(Revelation 22:2)*

It is very like Him to bring beautiful closure to the deepest scars of the human race. Because, you see, the damaging effects of the sinful fall-out that shattered the peace of the first garden are eventually reversed in the last—proving that He is more than aware of our need and has provided for every contingency.

You are so loved, friend. It was Love that first planted a garden.

When you have the chance to walk through a garden, breathe deeply. That pure, tree-manufactured oxygen was designed for your lungs' benefit. Open your eyes—those colors and textures were the driving force behind your retina's original blueprint. Let your ears discern the bird's song and the bee's flight—it was for this moment that its delicate inner workings were created. Feel the breeze and the sun on your skin—those dendrites and nerves were fused for this.

And open your heart-strings! The God who devised Eden is working to bring you at last to His heavenly garden, in triumph and joy!

The garden is an expression of God's personality, of His crazy love for us, if we will grasp its meaning. So when your heart is losing its fervor and what is fallen and corrupt blunts your spirit's song, head to the garden.

You may just find Love there . . .

Directionally Challenged

Have you ever been lost?

To the point where you had to ask for help? Or seek a map? Or surrender to tears and throw a hissy fit? Or hurl something at the nasty GPS that got you in your predicament in the first place?

I hope I am not the only one.

There is something about getting lost that makes you feel very—small. Your personal space shrinks like plastic on a flame when compared to the looming world with its incomprehensible enormity. There is something very visceral about the gorge of panic which rises in your throat at a busy intersection, when you have no idea whatever which direction to turn—and the anxiety is compounded immensely by the impatient locals honking in unison behind you, as you pause to take stock of your life.

Our GPS recently led my husband and me on a merry little chase in an unfamiliar city. We didn't realize that it switches automatically to a 'memory' function when the signal is lost—as it was when we parked underground. The unforeseen circumstance of the exit ramp we had entered being blocked for construction meant that we left the building on the opposite side.

Chaos ensued.

"Turn left at the next intersection," cooed our obliging mechanical navigator.

My husband was puzzled. "I don't think that's right," he mumbled, a bewildered shrug lifting his eyebrows. But he surrendered to the confidence of GPS Janet and turned left.

"Recalculating," interjected The Voice. "Turn right at North 33rd Street, followed by a left at 116th Avenue."

Both of us were somewhat surprised to read the sign for **South** 33rd Street scrolling past as we turned. The surprise turned to alarm and frustration as The Voice repeatedly called out instructions for streets which were non-existent on our present route.

Exasperated, Brent reached over and shut the GPS off.

After eventually inching our way to more familiar territory, I turned the unit back on, just for fun.

"Recalculating," GPS Janet murmured supportively. "Turn left at 105th Avenue."

By then, we were 5 miles from the city . . .

Faulty GPS units are not the only pitfall in our life manoeuvers. There are many ways in which we can be directionally challenged. For example, I sometimes forget which way is 'up'. And I can turn to my garden for some inspiration.

I can't tell you how many thousands of seeds I must have planted through the years. Seeds so tiny you need special tweezers and if you sneeze—poof! Seeds bumpy, rough, wrinkled, smooth and spherical, flat and hard and brittle. Seeds speckled and raven black and gangrenous green and bug-like. Each of them has its own peculiar germination rituals. Each requires specific and often very different growing conditions. Despite their differences, they all have one little habit in common.

Their roots go **down** and their shoots go **up**!

Unerringly, those root fibers somehow know to head for deeper ground, and the stems reach their leaves up to the sun with a single-minded determination which is awe inspiring! I have tried to mess them up. I have put them in 'upside down' and 'sideways'. I have dug them up and reinserted them in a new position and if that didn't mortally offend them, they corrected their course in a day or two and steadily asserted their directional focus undeterred by my GPS Janet-like creative license.

How very humbling to be set straight by a humble seed.

Even a seed knows that it must dedicate every ounce of energy into getting its leaves ever upward. Its very existence depends upon this function. Without the sun, its food factories grind to a halt. It forfeits its energy source, its inner clock, the obligatory ability to grow and reproduce and survive. And every day of its active life cycle, it presses upward, upward, always and forever upward.

How often I forget that the sun (Son!) is my life source, too. How often I am so busy looking down in the dirt or around at the weeds, that I miss those golden warm rays of love and support, energy and strength. If I am to survive, grow, function well, I desperately need to remember to look up!

> **"Search for the LORD and for His**
> **strength; continually seek Him."**
> **(Psalm 105:4)**

It is much easier to track the sun's route on a clear day, of course. On cloudy days, it is easy to forget that the sun is still there. But from God's lofty perspective, those cloudy circumstances that block Him from our view are small and so very temporary! They are simply a film of moisture, a wispy curtain dwarfed by the expanse of an infinite sky.

When I think of those tiny seeds and their inherent wisdom, I am encouraged to look up. Even under cloud cover, I know the sun is shining where God lives. And oh, how I need to remember that!

Lift your head, friend. Seek God with all your heart, soul, mind and strength. Directionally speaking, the right way is **up**!

(C'mon, are you going to be outwitted by a seed?)

To Prune, Or Not To Prune . . .

I don't know if my plants hate me for it or not, but I do it anyway. It's really for their own good, you see.

When I have a set of little seedlings coming along nicely, I do it. Before the sap flows in the apple trees in the spring, I do it. And all through the season when I see something amiss on a shrub here and there, I do it as well.

I'm talking pruning.

Just as tiny seedlings show some healthy growth, I pinch their tops off. I cut away stems that cross each other or that aren't pleasingly shaped on shrubs and trees. And my tomatoes get a healthy dose of snips when I see straggly stems growing where I don't want them.

I'm sure they don't like to see me coming at those times, with pruning shears in tow, or fingernails twitching with anticipation. It must be so frustrating to lose a part of yourself to the whim of someone else's design.

Ouch.

I mean well, I really do. With my developing store of gardening logic, I know that if left alone, shrubs will grow into unbalanced, gangly shapes that will deter them from producing a pleasing form in the future. My little seedlings will, from the stress of being nipped here and there, produce an extra vigorous, more compact branching structure that in the end will result in more and bigger blooms. And my tomatoes may produce less fruit, but each orb will be larger, tastier, and more suitably placed on the stems than if left to their own devices.

Do you sense a painful lesson approaching?

Sometimes God as Master Gardener needs to pinch us back, too. Maybe there are behavioral habits or thought patterns we have allowed to creep in and they simply must go in order for us to remain productive and healthy. Spiritual dead-weights, so to speak, that will choke out what otherwise potentially could develop into beautiful or delicious.

Even some things that are **good** must be cut away in order to make room for **best**. Like my tomatoes. Sometimes with God it isn't **quantity** but **quality** that really counts, so His pruning shears come out.

Snip.

> *"I am the true grapevine, and my Father is the gardener. He cuts off every branch of mine that doesn't produce fruit, and He prunes the branches that do bear fruit so they will produce even more. Yes, I am the vine; you are the branches. Those who remain in me, and I in them, will produce much fruit. For apart from me, you can do nothing."*
> *(John 15:1-2, 5)*

This pruning process isn't—well, comfortable. In fact, it can be downright painful to let go of parts of ourselves. A little pinch on that pride branch. A little snip at that stem of selfishness. A whack at that vine of self-reliance. It hurts to lose a goodly tendril of our own agendas and time lines and willful desires.

We have this tendency to glare at those lost branches on the ground in a futile attempt to will them back on. Our focus is so energetic in regarding the loss, we forget to tally the gain. Under stress, we can't see future potential as we count the cost. A microwave generation, we are addicted to the 'quick fix'. We want what we want and we want it now!

But **fruit** is the issue. I know when I pinch and trim in my garden that the loss is temporary and the gain is glorious! And so by faith I must assume that my benefit after this Triumphal Trim will be beyond my imagination. That God in His wisdom is planting something great within my heart.

So, **growth** or **comfort**?

Sigh.

Bring on the pruning shears! I want to be **amazing**!

HARDENED OFF

A greenhouse is the ideal place in which to grow plants, right? Nuh-uh!

A greenhouse is the ideal place to **start** plants. Temperature and humidity controlled, armed with automatic watering systems and friendly folks on hand to nip any troubles in the bud, it is the ideal environment to coax reluctant seeds into germinating and to give the resultant seedlings the best possible start in life.

Once the plants are off and running, the friendly folks in charge like to get them ready for the 'real world'. The little plant-lings will get spindly and distorted if they aren't introduced to some opposition—in moderation, of course. Fans are set up to mimic 'wind'. Temperatures are gradually cooled to create an environment that more closely resembles the outdoors.

Even so, when gardeners in this area buy greenhouse plants, we know that we must 'harden them off' when we get them home or they won't survive the transition from hothouse to cold spring soil.

Coddled vegetation has been accustomed to an ideal indoor climate. When faced with cool night temperatures, unpredictable winds, occasional dry spells, and the full-strength version of the hot prairie sun, plants can throw a fit and go into 'yardiac arrest'. They need a few days of gradual acclimatization to their new location, beginning with a few hours a day in a sheltered spot, working toward full exposure to the elements. Thus 'hardened off', they will grow on to greatness and add splendor or flavor wherever they are planted.

Oh, boy. Can you see where I'm going with this?

People, too, need hardening off. Ideally we start life in the greenhouse of a loving home, where gradually we are safely exposed to more and more of real life. We are allowed to make mistakes and experience positive and negative consequences, getting accustomed to the outside world under the guidance of our parents. Mentally, emotionally, physically, and spiritually, we need time to mature in a protected place before taking on the challenges of the adult world.

But if we are allowed to grow completely sheltered, we develop selfish habits which twist our potential. Without some opposition, we have no need to cultivate a strong backbone. If we remain constantly and perfectly well-watered, we may never expand our root system.

Accordingly, the Master Gardener applies 'hardening off' principles of His own. He knows that the little things that cause us grief—catching a cold, getting caught in traffic, losing our wallets—are invaluable baby-steps toward enlarging the skills and resourcefulness crucial to surviving more serious life-storms.

The realities of a fallen world are harsh. Wounds are sooner or later inevitable for us all—the death of a spouse, a failed marriage, an estranged relationship, a nasty medical diagnosis. And while none of these were in God's original plan, He is ever-ready to help us through them! He knows very well that the compassion, endurance, faithfulness, patience, and character that are planted in our hearts—seeded in the confines of a greenhouse—only develop their full flavor when encountering painfully adverse conditions.

He sees what you **can** be—and will allow what is necessary to draw out your most beautiful blooms!

"I have told you all this so that you may have peace in
me. Here on earth you will have many trials and sorrows.
But take heart, because I have overcome the world."
(John 16:33)

Maybe you are in the middle of being 'hardened off". It feels pretty nasty, doesn't it? I know—I have been there, too. Rest assured, the Master Gardener knows exactly what you need and will only introduce you to what is absolutely crucial for your growth. He knows the exact speed of that nasty windstorm ahead—and will give you preparatory steps to ready for it. He can see the season of frost next month—and will expand your skills to ward it off with as little loss as possible. He will show you how to endure until the next rainfall by teaching you how to dig your roots down deep in His promises and stand tall and strong in His Truth.

Take heart! Instead of resenting the process, can you learn to welcome and embrace it? Tall order, I know, but necessary to your peace of mind.

Because when you are properly 'hardened off', you can take that step out of the greenhouse and bloom where you are planted.

And not only will you survive any adverse conditions that arise—you'll **thrive** there!

Wow. You're looking good . . .

Fertilizer Frenzy

Grow big or don't bother, I always say.

(Well, okay, I don't exactly say it quite like that. Put that way, it sounds pretty silly, really.)

What I mean is, in a geographical location with such hindrances as wind-chills down to -50°C, no guarantee of any month of our year being fully frost-free, a ridiculously short growing season, a plethora of insect pests, wind and soil-born diseases, and a tendency toward either drought or flood (sometimes both during one growing season!) you've got to make hay while the sun shines.

In other words, **git goin'**.

To bring out all that my plants can possibly offer in such conditions, I rely on fertilizer. And not just one kind! I use anything I can to jump-start my tender seedlings from start to finish, in order to make the most of the harsh environment.

Fertilizer frenzy . . .

I rely on a super-charged plant-starter formula for my seedlings. It promises to develop a strong vital root system which in turn assures a good growth cycle and plenty of potential as the plants mature. I use a rich compost material to supplement the soil around my perennials. I apply a different fertilizer blend to my tomatoes. Another yet to my blueberries. And still another to my flower pots to stimulate lots of annual color.

But I know the potential danger to 'lay it on a little thick'. Overkill, if you will. In fact, if I applied all of the products that I normally would apply during a growing season all at once, it would be a gardening catastrophe.

One that would seriously maim most, and kill the rest stone dead.

Oops.

In my early, 'green' days I once killed an entire tray of beautiful little seedlings in my fervor to fertilize. The super-charged jump-start type of fertilizer that advertised such great results burned my little plants' leaves right off. The concoction which should have served as steroids actually dried them to a crisp. When I re-read the label, I realized that the product was never to be applied to young leaves because of the tendency to scorch tender growth.

More oops.

Delicate young plants can't handle the power of unbridled input. They must be exposed to good things in small amounts and at regular intervals (rather like being 'hardened off'). In the same way, if I over-applied fertilizer to my older and established perennial beds, much would be a wasted investment; only what the roots can readily handle and use will be pulled up into the plant's system. The rest either oxidizes into the air or feeds weeds. And I sure don't want to be doing **that**.

Misdirected fertilizer frenzy has also played into my desire to lengthen the growing season. Applying products too late in the year for the short-term goal of seeing more lovely tendrils grow in the fall on my grape vines, I sacrificed the long-term aim of strong plants who are hardened off for the winter. Putting their resources into a wild late-season surge above-ground, they hadn't enough time to store vital energy for the inclement weather to come.

They didn't live to see another spring.

I'm so glad that God doesn't get in a frenzied panic to see me to my final potential. He never douses me with more than I can handle at the time. He then leaves me a 'soaking period', where I can mull over lessons learned and begin to apply them to my life to the best of my ability at that time in my growth cycle. His fertilizer is a timed-release formula, drawing me along in my development bit by bit, root by shoot, spread out safely over a lifetime of gradual intake, with long-term results. He **never sacrifices long-term gain for short-term triumph!**

What a good God, this Master Gardener of my heart!

> *"But grow in the grace and knowledge of*
> *our Lord and Savior Jesus Christ. To Him be*
> *glory both now and forever! Amen."*
> *(II Peter 3:18 NIV)*

Knowing my end from my beginning, what nutrients I lack, my fruiting potential, and when the next rain will come, He oh, so gently directs and oversees my growth in His kingdom. He uses the fertilizers of neediness and dependency to sink my roots deep in His resources. He applies the mulch of drought and difficulty to drive my thirst toward His sustenance. He waters in the rich food of unexpected trials to stretch my ability to take in His Word's Truth.

And I grow . . .

No frenzy. Just solid, dependable, steady progress.

Ready. Set.

Grow!

Dug Up

I knew it was wrong, but I couldn't help myself. Compelled by a curiosity I couldn't deny, I did it again.

I dug up a seed.

I know, I know. Once tucked into the soil, seeds are best left to themselves. Alone in the dark, moist earth, they magically swell with potential. They put down root so shoot can burst toward the sun in triumph. And the process is definitely thwarted if someone (a nosy, impatient gardener, for example) interrupts by digging it up again.

But by the time spring planting season arrives, I want green and I want it now! When I check the trays, I fret. It's been like—a day or two already! Where are the plants? Hovering over my seed trays several times a day in eager anticipation, I watch for any sign that a seedling is pushing its way to the surface, peering at every bump and crack for clues to show that something is happening under there, where those seeds are buried.

Impatient, I scratch the soil where a seed should be, and grunt with satisfaction when I find it. Frowning, I see that it is just beginning to swell. No root tip yet. I recover it in its earthy grave. Choosing another cell, I scratch again. This time, a gleam of white is revealed. Enthralled, I work too fast, uncovering the life I have found clumsily, rashly.

The tiny root snaps off the seed. I have killed it in my haste to ascertain its progress. Dismayed, I push it back in place, as if covering up my mistake will allow it to resume its fragile commencement. Talk about denial.

Sighing, I retrieve my seed packet and replant that seed cell, vowing to never again disturb the miracle taking place. Knowing myself so well, I realize that it will only take a day or two, and I will be back again, eagerly grubbing around to see if there really truly is growth happening among the rows and rows I have sown.

In the garden of my heart, am I any different? Impatiently awaiting change, how many times have I interfered in the process, sabotaging the tender impetus for growth by my bungling?

Hmmmm . . .

Sometimes God works in secret, deep, buried places within us. The change and growth are delicate and 'underground', so to speak. In these dark, unknown places He is working to produce the optimum conditions for faith-roots to grow and develop—long before any obvious transformation can be seen in our habits, speech, reactions, or desires.

Always impatient, I want to see immediate results as soon as any new seed of knowledge or insight is tucked into my heart and mind. I want to reach my full potential today. (Actually, yesterday would have been better!) Time is too precious to waste in waiting for some unknown process to take root somewhere where I can't see it, let alone control it. If there is no outward sign, it hurts to feel that I am stuck in one place, stagnating, not maturing or moving ahead.

And yet, whether I see it or not, God is at work! In fact, in the words of Jesus, **"My Father is always working, and so am I." (John 5:17)** Ever gentle, ever mindful of what we need most and what will work best for our unique personalities in our unique circumstances, He is planting ideas, inspiration, courage, integrity, truth—the embryo of His own character deep within us. If we water it with a generous dose of His Word, soak it in prayer, and turn our faces to the Son, He will do the rest.

> *"And I am certain that God, who began a good work*
> *within you, will continue His work until it is finally*
> *finished on the day when Christ Jesus returns."*
> *(Philippians 1:6)*

Even when I am afraid that the growth is not happening, that I have somehow fallen off track, there are tiny tendrils of roots invisibly expanding. When the time is right, any steps I've taken to allow God to build a strong base beneath my feet will show in the fruit I can produce. My tendency to second-guess the process and what God as Master Gardener is doing in my life, my arrogance in assuming that I can do better than He, only undermine the good work He is trying to accomplish in His own way, His own time.

So wait. Let your faith grow, knowing that the Master Gardener is on the job.

And no digging!

Clematis Comeback

Let me tell you about my Clematis comeback.

It's funny, really. *Now*. At the time, I was definitely not laughing. I wasn't crying, either, in case you heard otherwise. (The official report is that my allergies were acting up . . .) But many months after the fact, I can see the humor.

I **think** that's what you call it . . .

It all started with our garage project. My main flower garden was designed directly behind the garage, so I was aware of the potential risk when it was time to pull the old down to make room for the new. The plan was to build a few feet further north so that there would be a buffer zone and the least damage to existing shrubs and perennials as possible.

Ha, ha.

My husband, being an early riser, had the old garage down completely before I got up. Concerned, I ran out to survey the heap of rubble the tractor and he had managed to produce. The concern had grown into shock and dismay a few minutes later, once I had a chance to see for myself what had happened.

A lovely clematis vine had been growing on a metal trellis on the back of the old garage. My husband Brent had affixed it to the wall to give it more stability—a very kind gesture from a non-gardener, I thought at the time.

Imagine my surprise when I saw that the garage had been completely flattened, with the clematis still attached.

Let me give you a clear visual on this—my hapless clematis was pulled out by the roots, a blooming purple profusion, lying at an impossibly awkward angle, clinging stubbornly to a completely mangled trellis which tenaciously remained screwed to the vinyl siding of a wall crushed beyond recognition.

My allergies kicked in at that precise moment.

To give myself some credit, I didn't whine (too much). I refrained from shooting him the 'look' (after the first few days). I knew that there was nothing I could do, so I mourned in private (to anyone who would listen) and moved on with my life.

The new garage took shape. There was indeed a minimum of disruption to the rest of my prized plant collection (Brent being by now well-afraid of the consequences). Spring was overtaken by summer, and both were clematis free. I purchased a new specimen and placed it on a lovely iron sculpture in the middle of my circular rose garden and life resumed its summery pace.

And then, out of the blue, I saw it.

I couldn't believe my eyes.

That crazy clematis was growing, back from the dead. For a few days I checked and re-checked, in case it was a new rogue weed variety that just *looked* a lot like a clematis vine. In a week, it was decidedly healthy. In a month, I reclaimed the twisted mangled trellis corpse from the junk pile, straightened it best as I could, and trained the first little viny tendrils around its humbled posts.

Unbelievable.

The Phoenix rises . . .

And somehow, this silly little human (and plant) drama has encouraged me. Taught me to hope. Prepared me for a life's journey of ups and downs, failures and triumphs, ebbs and flows. Been for me a kind of miniature instruction manual on resilience.

Given me eyes to see beyond the skin of what is, to what can and will be.

Because if a silly old plant can rise from the ashes of a war zone—er, construction site—after many years of growth were ripped from the ground, maybe I can survive my life-wounds, too. Maybe regeneration and healing are possible. The mystery of this clematis, come back from the dead, plants an inner hint that set-backs are temporary and beauty is forever—and my heart pounds with a delicious tremor that beats hope, hope, hope.

You see, it reminds me of One who conquered death completely. Into infinity.

For me.

"In His great mercy, He has given us new birth into a living hope through the resurrection of Jesus Christ from the dead, and into an inheritance that can never perish, spoil, or fade—kept in heaven for you, who through faith are shielded by God's power until the coming of the salvation that is ready to be revealed in the last time.

In this you greatly rejoice, though now for a little while you may have had to suffer grief in all kinds of trials. These have come so that your faith—of greater worth than gold, which perishes even though refined by the fire—may be proved genuine and may result in praise, glory and honor when Jesus Christ is revealed."
(I Peter 1:3-7 NIV)

Has your upward momentum been ripped out by the roots? Have dreams close to your heart been crushed and left to die in a mangled mess? Take heart, friend.

What God plants, grows. What fire refines, glows. So—shoulders back. Head up. Knees bent. Prayers out.

It's time for a clematis comeback . . .

Bring On The Son!

Have you ever tried to mess with a plant?

I mean, really mess with it? Get into its head space and turn its world upside down?

I have—in my primary classroom. Almost every year, my students and I try something crazy to see if we can disturb a plant's regular old life, and it's surprising how easy it actually is.

One of the most dramatic things we have done is to cover a plant with a paper bag, set it in a sunny window, water it well, and watch. It gets weird, fast.

It's downright shocking how quickly things turn nasty for the poor creature. First, almost imperceptibly, it wilts. Then it **fades.** Yes, fades—its color leaches away in a species of shamed slink. Then its form goes all wonky—it begins to twist and swoop at unreasonable angles, like it is searching desperately for something (which it is, of course). Once leaves begin to drop off you know its system is failing.

It has been forced to cut off useless appendages in a last-ditch effort to survive. (Rather like a person's extremities shut down in a case of hypothermia in order to keep the integrity of the core intact.)

When it positively lies down on the ground a weak, pale shadow of its former self, you know the messing is over.

As a scientific proof to small children that every living plant needs the sun to survive, this caper hasn't an equal. And I wonder whether our entire society needs a simple controlled experiment to wake us up to an equally true spiritual reality.

You need the Son, my friend.

Oh, you'll do all right at first—just a little pale. Just a wee bit weak compared to some of the vibrant souls in your vicinity. You'll shove that rebellious thought down deep and laugh it off and firmly fix your layer of self-protectionism, sealing your heart off in a safe little paper bag.

When your soul screams for more and begins to twist out of shape in its growingly frantic search for the unknown ingredient that it craves, you'll look at other twisted forms around you and label yourself 'normal'. Losing touch by now with which way is up, your entire frame gets bent out of shape in its prowling for answers. Trying a little of this, a little of that—counterfeits, if you will, that bring temporary pleasure or serve to dull your senses to the initial reasons for the search.

You will barely notice that you are little by little losing your very self. Now your system goes into full survival mode and you begin to accept this life as your new normal—wake up, get through the day, collapse exhausted. Repeat. Repeat *ad nauseum* . . .

And you lie down and give up, a pale shadow of who you were meant to be . . .

All for the lack of Sonshine in your life.

Yeah, okay, it sounds a little dramatic. But friends, I, who was raised to know God, have been there! In the midst of great teaching, solid habits, prayer and self-discipline, I had built just enough of a barrier, my personal paper bag, that it blocked me from the very One I needed most to survive. And not just survive—**thrive!** I didn't know that in all the 'religious activity' all I needed was to bask in the Son! To have personal contact, Heart to heart, drinking in the life that is truly Life!

Not being accustomed to this strong Sonshine, I sometimes run back to my paper bag. It is 'safe'—I know that world. I sometimes buy the lie that it is better in there, where the Light doesn't hurt my eyes! But I am beginning to see that this place of light and hope and brightness is where my strength comes from, where I become what my soul most craves, where an inner beauty is forged on the nectar that His rays stir in my veins, where something holy and pure and true is photosynthesized.

And I feel my backbone straighten from its impossible curves and in the pain of the straightening I see what I **could** be!

> *". . . God has given us eternal life, and this life is in*
> *His Son. He who has the Son has life; he who does*
> *not have the Son of God does not have life."*
> *(I John 5:11-12 NIV)*

I thought I knew this God of my youth. I did, to a point. But trouble has a way of clearing the clutter, of removing the 'paper bags', so to speak. With enhanced vision I see that this God, this radiant Son, wants my permission to draw even closer, ever deeper into my world, where within my small and weak frame can be planted a Light so pure and true it takes my breath away. He wants to **belong** to me—to be everything I need.

No more baggy barriers.

Bring on the Son!

Only The Best

My husband Brent put the finishing touches on my 'garden' room, a narrow space lined with windows and bursting with light at the south end of the new garage. The potting bench he installed sprawled across its entire width. Full of joyful anticipation, I bought the seeds that would become the plants that would fill the room in the back of the garage that Brent built.

Slowly, the rows of trays and potting soil acquired a sheen of green. Slowly, slowly, roots branched and stems arched and leaves unfurled and tendrils vined. There was only one exception.

That exception was my tray of morning glories. A new color variety that I had never grown, I waited for these with an especially hopeful heart. Daily—no, many times a day—I anxiously checked the barren soil for a glimpse of something, anything, that would tell me that the glory had arrived.

Days went by and only a very few seeds had germinated. While other plants were developing beautifully, my morning glories were lagging. Germination was spotty at best—and growth was pitiful in the extreme.

I had carefully and correctly nicked the seed coat on each rock-hard seed to speed germination. I had monitored the temperature diligently, both day and night.

They languished.

I ensured the proper proportions of light, soil moisture and nutrient availability, and still they languished. If they did germinate, it was to remain stuck at the cotyledon stage, wearing nothing but their original 'baby leaves', silently stunted.

An investigative visit to a greenhouse was in order. When I got to the morning glory aisle, I saw them—easily trailing two feet long, massive leaves twining enthusiastically all along the vines. Disturbed, I asked an employee when they had been planted.

Her answer? The same week as mine! "They grow so easily once they have germinated," she shared pleasantly.

I came to a startling conclusion after double-checking the facts.

The seed was . . . bad, somehow.

After offering the optimum and getting the bare minimum, there had to have been something awry with the seed itself. I cast my mind back to where I had purchased them and recalled that I had grabbed them off of a sale rack at a 'non-gardening' store.

Sheesh.

How often have I planted poor quality in my own heart because it was convenient? 'On sale', as it were? Readily available in the wrong place? A temptation for the senses with its bright and flashy packaging, promising results it could not deliver?

How often have I invested in poor, or even 'okay', when in my short growing season, I only have room for the **best?**

Only the best. My heart's garden deserves it, you see.

God's Word promises higher, stronger, deeper, and more abundant. Greener, fuller, absolutely bursting with potential, dripping with promise, brimming with harvest-hope. And time after time, I head with mule-like obstinacy to the sales rack, to the quick fix, to the temporary escape from the pain that drives us all.

Father, forgive me, for I don't know what I do . . .

We go to great lengths to attain the best for our offices, corporations, kitchens, recreational activities. We haunt the techie aisles in the department stores so we can keep up with the ever-changing market. Our appliances gleam with the latest advancements. And we ignore our hearts' needs and stuff them full of temporary garbage that will never ever satisfy—and wonder why we remain empty.

Father, forgive us, for we don't know what we do . . . .

"Guard your heart above all else, for it
determines the course of your life."
(Proverbs 4:23)

To guard your heart means to offer it **only the best** . . . and the best is not working harder, or shopping more. Not food or booze or any other temporary gratification. Not earning more or making more friends or excelling in your profession or getting a pat on the back for something you did that will be forgotten when the patting is over. It's not even praying oftener or serving God with added energy or reading your Bible more, although of course those are all good things. But done with the wrong motivation, out of obligation, such disciplines can leave you just as dry as when you came. (I know because I've done it!)

In order to plant the best, you need to find the feet of Jesus and stay there. Soak Him in. Let your heart drink fully the presence of the living God. Allow your deepest core needs to be fully met in the mystery of simply **being**.

This search will take all your resolve. The carrot at the end of the stick will often elude you. Your quest may take you into unfamiliar waters. But my friends, you must try. For the sake of your heart, it is your only option.

Unless you are satisfied with lagging, awkward growth and frustrated fruit production, only the **best** will do.

And the **best** is **Jesus** . . .

Radical Raspberry Recommendation

Raspberries are so delicious, aren't they?

My raspberry patch is a large one and produces abundantly. Well, most years, anyway. There was one year in which we got none.

As in ZERO. An almost miraculous feat, considering how heavily they usually produce. (Did I emphasize the word 'abundant' enough?)

And it all came about because of a radical raspberry recommendation.

This Raspberry Saga begins one early spring. Raspberries are **biennial** plants. This means in effect that they grow one year, produce fruit in the second year, and then die back. Meanwhile, they 'sucker'—produce new plants on sucker shoots growing on the roots of the originals. Every year, a healthy patch contains both actively fruiting plants, and yearling plants which will themselves sucker and produce fruit the following year.

Early spring is the time to 'cane' your raspberries. There is a mass of last year's fruiting stock which is now dead, and needs to be removed, or 'caned', growing intertwined with the present year's fruit-bearing plants. Caning, while not strictly necessary, is desirable because of the dead canes' dry bristles and thorns. Any unsuspecting harvester trying to pick the fruit is scratched unmercifully; often the scratches turn into nasty red welts.

It is worth the effort to shed these prickly scourges, let me tell you.

Here's the catch—due to these thorns, the caning process is **not** my favorite job. Some of the old canes come out peacefully with demure shrugs, but many put up a cantankerous protest, making the task all the more difficult. So when we got our radical raspberry recommendation, we decided to give it a try.

My husband had done some business with a 'snaggle-toothed' trucker (his words, not mine) and had received a fascinating tidbit of information that went something like this—if you did it early enough in the season, you could actually light your raspberry patch on fire. The fire would consume the dry dead canes and leave the fresh green ones intact to produce berries uninhibited by the snarl of undergrowth.

In theory, an interesting prospect.

My husband was willing to experiment. I was reluctant, but if it meant I didn't have to jump into the nasty scratchy bushes, who was I to complain too rigorously?

One fine spring day, he lit the patch. Several times.

And nothing happened. The patch refused to light at all.

Convinced that it was 'fate', I turned back toward the house. Behind me, there was a tremendous **'whump'** noise. I spun around to see wicked flames in an eight-foot high wall obliterating the entire raspberry patch. This was no crackling, merry, wiener-roast fire. This was a fiery inferno of death and doom like no other I had ever seen. It threw a preposterous amount of heat. It positively **roared**.

And then, as quickly as it had started, it was over.

And so were my raspberries . . .

To give the trucker some credit, it did effectively remove the old canes. But it also took the present year's growth. And with it, the entire season's fruit potential.

We never ate a single raspberry all summer.

Have you heeded the advice of any 'snaggle-toothed truckers' in your life?

We are so quick to offer advice. "Your baby looks like he could use some solid food—*my* baby did at that age." "You should try x-product—it did wonders for my brother-in-law." "That chiropractor in town is no good—you should try so and so instead."

And those are in the most part fairly innocuous. Then there are the radical raspberry recommendations. These are all the more radical because they are so sly and insidious. They are often not even spoken aloud—they are insinuated, hinted at—and the media tops the list of offenders.

"If you drink our product, you will join this talented, youthful, beautiful group of people and truly belong for the first time in your life."

"When you smooth this cream onto your face, your wrinkles will disappear and you will get the life you've always dreamed of."

"Tired of watching everyone else live the good life? Invest with us. Buy our lottery tickets. Buy our book on how to triple your income overnight . . . ."

Blah, blah, blah . . .

If you don't evaluate the source, you just might go up in flames. And they won't be the crackling, merry, wiener-roast kind.

Jesus dared to claim, "*I am the way, the truth, and the life.*" *(John 14:6 NIV)* He boldly sets Himself as the ultimate standard for what is true, right, good, authentic, and satisfying. This means that anything else that claims otherwise is—**not** true, right, good, authentic, or satisfying. Not in the long run.

Whoa. What a lot of radical raspberry recommendations are running around out there . . .

Don't get burned.

You can trust Jesus—**His** radical recommendations will produce richly satisfying results!

The Forgetfulness Factor

My memory is like a sieve.

Except that rather than retaining the desirable and tossing the remainder, only the unwanted and the useless get trapped in its aging mesh. I can remember jingles from my Sesame Street days, but details such as where I planted what—those tend to get flushed down the drain. A little like throwing out the baby with the bathwater.

Hence my passion for plant tags.

Plant tags are to gardeners what computer geeks are to NASA—pretty much indispensable. When I am planting my rows and rows of tender flowering annuals in rows and rows of trays on my potting bench in the spring, I plant markers with as much assiduity as seeds. Many specimens, especially those in the same family, tend to look a lot like their neighbors at the seedling stage.

At one point, many of the tender little critters have either a close affinity to grass, or bear a striking resemblance to helicopter rotors.

When I seed my garden, I usually experiment with plant pairings—puttingrowsinjuxtapositionforthepurposesofdiscouraging pests, for example. At the time, I am so certain the pairing is brilliant. But before the wispy seedlings emerge, I have forgotten what that species of brilliance was.

Hence the plant tags.

And it isn't only me. There are entire companies in existence to feed the appetite of gardeners for labels. Check the internet—you'll be astounded by the variety and quantity of labels you can order for yourself if you have a current credit card.

I was at a bridal shower once and I actually won a game—a rarity for me. When I saw what I had won, I didn't know whether to laugh or cry.

It was a plaque engraved with the words "*I Don't Remember Planting This!*" I wanted to laugh because it confirmed the fact that I was not alone. I wanted to cry because I had a sneaking suspicion that the game may have been rigged . . .

I posted it beside a batch of pink lilies, whose species name has—er, slipped my mind.

Let's face it—we humans tend to be forgetful. And we tend to project that trait undeservedly, naively, onto God Himself.

Even in Isaiah's day, the people were complaining that **"[t]he Lord has forsaken me, the Lord has forgotten me."**

God's response? **"Can a mother forget the baby at her breast and have no compassion on the child she has borne? Though she may forget, I will not forget you! See, I have engraved you on the palms of my hands . . ." (Isaiah 49:14b-16a NIV)**

How infinitely tender. How surpassingly sweet.

When we get something engraved, it represents something extra special—a gift to mark a graduation, a wedding, or an anniversary. A piece of memorabilia to commemorate an award accomplished or a feat achieved. It embodies something we know we cannot afford to forget—like the remonstrance engraved on my garden sundial to 'Count Only Sunny Hours'.

Our names (and lives) are infinitely valuable to the Master Gardener. A deep desire to honor the occasion of your birth spurred the Holy Ruler of the Universe to engrave you on His palms. Those palms were scarred deeply by the engraving, but the marks carved there ensure that you will remain His forever. They represent a permanent physical love-link from His heart to yours. An invisible tie stronger than death itself stretches arm-wide on a cross that was brutally stained—and then left behind, empty, in the brilliance of unsurpassed victory.

When the circumstances of your life blind you to what has already been made indelible, look up. Visualize the skin scarred by the tracing of your name, and take heart.

God knows we are forgetful. As well as He knows He is not.

But to forever silence the forgetfulness factor in our own minds, He resorts to something we can relate to in His desire to plant a calm, peaceful assurance into our feeble fluttering.

He writes you down. Permanently.

He will not forget . . .

Busy Bees

Bees are amazing.

Stingers aside, of course.

Roaming from flower to flower, they set up a steady hum of activity in my garden. They are the first among their fellow creatures to enjoy the revitalized world after winter's cold grip loses its strength.

As soon as there are blossoms, there are bees.

One of the best places to be on a warm spring day is beneath my apple tree. The scent is intoxicating. The buzzing is a sure signal that all is well with the world. That industry and hard work really do pay off. That the microcosm of this fruiting habitat is in balance. That after a pleasant summer, apples will be sure to follow.

Tireless in their determination, these busy fellows have blossom on the brain. Seek, stick, and spread is their motto. For months, they single-mindedly trace and retrace their paths through the potential candidates in their vicinity.

'Did I miss that one? Better just check to make sure.'

'Have I spread pollen over in that corner yet? Hmmm—might need help with all this.'

While their missives are likely not in English, we know that communication is among their strong points.

A bee's work ethic is another skill near the top of the list. Constantly on the move, heeding the directions of their revered Queen, bees embody a cult-like standard of disciplined rank, efficient protocols, and dedication to the hive.

We could learn a lot from bees.

If we consider for a moment that the hive is similar to the global church, and bees' obedience similar to us carrying out the orders of our Leader, there are actually a lot of interesting parallels. There are a number of cues we could take from our insect brethren.

First, they know what their job is. They are gathering and spreading pollen.

Do we know what our job is?

Second, they are not easily deterred from their mission. With a determination that puts most of us to shame, they attack their daily drill with gusto.

In addition, they are clearly aware of who calls the shots in the hive. They don't ever seem to rebel or set up their own agendas or fight over which one needs to go where, or why. They simply follow the directions given, and carry out Her Highness' orders to the best of their abilities. Their stingers are used in emergencies, not to prove their point or drive others away. And they hum in pleasure as they work . . .

Oh, boy.

Maybe if we had the understanding that without our spreading the good news of our Master Gardener, all the spiritual fruit in the world would cease production, we would take His commission more seriously. No pollen, no yummy fruit. No fruit, no trees. No trees, no oxygen. No oxygen, no life . . .

Wow. Hadn't thought of it quite like that before . . .

Friends, it is time to gather to our hives in unity. Time to work tirelessly together to spread the news of what our God has done for us. Time to fulfill the greatest commission ever conferred on any band of soldiers.

Jesus said in *Matthew 28:18-20—"I have been given all authority on heaven and on earth."* (That means He is King of the hive!)*" Therefore, go and make disciples of all the nations, baptizing them in the name of the Father and the Son and the Holy Spirit. Teach these new disciples to obey all the commands I have given you."* (There is our job description!) *"And be sure of this: I am with you always, even to the end of the Age."* (There is the source of the 'gusto' we need to fulfill our task!)

Yes, we could learn a lot from bees.

I could learn a lot from bees. This lesson is a steep challenge to my own heart. I have not lived as a bee should, I am afraid. I have often thought myself clever enough to manage on my own, without the Commander, without the hive. I have rejected my job description and sought other tasks, easier tasks, ones more suited to pleasure and self.

Lord, give me the courage to regain my lost destiny! Plant within my heart the desire to serve you as I ought.

Lord, give us the power to live as busy bees . . .

SUMMER

". . . a time to build up."
—*Ecclesiastes 3:3*

"We often miss opportunity because it's dressed in overalls and looks like work."
—*Thomas Edison*

Pot-Bound

With the onset of summer, the garden work begins in earnest. A big part of that work includes preparing and watering those high-maintenance mavens of the yard—pots. They add vibrancy and color to dark corners, showcase unusual or exotic specimens, and provide the enthusiast with an opportunity to let loose their own particular creative flair.

A stunning array of pots can be found on display at garden stores. They are made out of just about anything, from terracotta to plastic to iron to a new generation of fake super-plastics designed to look like the real thing, and priced to match. Each has its claim to fame—improved drainage or durable, lightweight design. Many are chip and frost-resistant. Astonishing hues enhance form and function. With an artistic eye, you can match plant to pot in a marriage of texture and color and shape, making the difference between dull and WOW!

When a plant outgrows its pot, especially if the pot is a favorite, I leave it for as long as I can. (Will I find the right replacement? Will it blow my year's gardening budget all in one fell swoop?) But when the plant actually looks like it is 'un-growing' itself, it's time for action before it gets too pot-bound.

Roots, ever seeking out new avenues of exploration, can begin circling the confines of a too-small pot, eventually growing in on themselves. We call this being 'root-bound' or 'pot-bound'. This spells trouble for the inmate of the pot.

Pot-bound plants have a distinctly egocentric focus. If you wait too long, even if a new, roomier pot is selected for the plant to be transferred into, the root system can become compromised. The gardener will have to take a sharp tool and 'score' the roots, cutting some of the overgrowth away, hoping to stimulate new, healthier growth.

Yikes!

People, too, need room to grow, to explore new territory, to plumb new depths in relationships or proficiency or personal goals. So many of us condemn our hearts to small pots because it is what we are used to. They feel safer than the other-world with its big unknown spaces. We get hurt and accept compromised growth and stunted sensibilities, just to maintain the status quo. Not able to extend mercy to ourselves or others, we end up circling around the same old places of misunderstanding and confusion and habit and pain. We let fear rob our choices. We stay rooted to the spot . . .

Pot-bound.

Change takes a lot of courage. Sometimes it hurts to dream bigger, to take chances, to grow in grace or faith. Growth involves risk. Rest assured that the Master Gardener sees the problem more fully than we. He knows that unless He cuts something away from our roots that is becoming redundant or inwardly biased, He won't have the working room to achieve what is best for our development. We will forfeit forward momentum—and the very beauty and fruitfulness we so desire.

"No eye has seen, no ear has heard, and
no mind has imagined what God has
prepared for those who love Him."
(I Corinthians 2:9b)

A root-job can definitely hurt. It can slow down growth for a while until we recover. We might need to practice allowing ourselves time to explore new options and avenues, new space for new roots.

But the 'pot' selected by your personal Garden Designer—the living space He prearranged for you—is just right to accentuate your personality, highlight your talents, and spur you to the place of abundance He visualizes in His mind's eye. It has been made of a phenomenal and revolutionary state-of-the-art material. Its finish is a more brilliant shade and shine than you have ever seen, because it was dreamed up in the brain of God Himself. It will be something beyond your expectations and imagination.

And it will showcase your beauty to perfection.

Don't stay bound to a pot that was yesterday's news. Risk a root run into the territory of God's leading. Scary—of course. But healthy? Unquestionably.

Now—get ready to bloom!

I Can Tell Where You've Been

I have a propensity to mimic people.

I don't consciously try to—it just happens! My ears seem to pick up the diction and tones and accent of those I have been hanging around with for a while. I even seem to suck up other people's mannerisms. People close to me can tell sometimes who I have been with, just by listening to me talk.

Weird, right?

Sooner or later, after spending time with someone, my mouth spouts words that sound like them—a Southern drawl, a Russian clip, a cockney swagger. Most of the time, it's good for a laugh. It makes storytelling in my classroom a pay-per-view event.

I think I missed my life's calling with the CIA. Sometimes I think that I would have made a good foreign agent.

Or chameleon.

Similarly, when I have spent some time in my garden, there is definitive evidence left behind on my person to show where I have been. In fruit season, my hands are stained a beautiful 'berry of the day' shade. In lily season, my calf, thigh, or hip, sport the unmistakable orange-gold pollen from one of the 40+ Asiatic lily varieties bordering the many pathways of my flower garden. In pruning season, I likely have some brier scratches somewhere on my arms. In just about any season, the old fingernail check would give the whole show away.

But most tell-tale of all are my knees.

I kneel a lot in my garden. Hoes are great for weeding, but they don't discriminate very well between the weed and the wanted. So down I go to get good and close to the botanical traitors and yank them out by hand to protect the integrity of what I want left standing. While planting, I love to kneel in warm, loose soil as I tuck in my bedding plants. Berry-picking, tending to tomatoes, laying more flat rocks for my landscaping projects—all are tended to on my knees.

This makes for an obvious smudge of irrefutable gardening evidence ever clinging to my leg-joints . . .

What if we as believers showed just as much tangible evidence when we have spent time in our heart's garden, with the Master Gardener Himself? What would be the signs that we had just been in God's presence, hanging out with Him, picking up His attributes, His manner of speech, His attitudes, His heart?

Makes one think, doesn't it?

In the Old Testament, Moses went to talk to God every day and write down anything He might dictate, to pass it on to his people. When he came away, his face was radiant. Wow. The people could tell whenever Moses had been spending time with God because his face literally glowed in the aftermath.

Oh, boy. Looks like I have to spend **way** more time in my heart's garden . . .

What a great goal for the season ahead—to spend enough time with God Himself that my very character, habits, responses, thought processes, and even physical self would all reflect where I had been.

Can you imagine a community of believers whose faces shine with God's own love and character? A group whose knees proved to the world that some serious prayer had just taken place? People would be beating down the church door to see what was going on.

And notice the difference to traditional teaching: this is not about **doing** more, **accomplishing** more, **preparing** more, **working** more—it is about **being** more. Simply staying in God's presence has the power to utterly transform us.

Moses had to veil his face so his people wouldn't freak out, back in the day.

> *"But whenever someone turns to the Lord, the veil is taken away. So all of us who have had the veil removed can see and reflect the glory of the Lord. And the Lord—who is the Spirit—makes us more and more like Him as we are changed into His glorious image."*
> *(II Corinthians 3: 16, 18)*

Whoa. Wouldn't it be cool if the next person you met today tipped her head on one side and said with an appraising glance, "I can sure tell where **you** have been!"

Yup. That peaceful glow really gives it away.

(And is that a smudge of *prayer pollen* on your left knee?)

Hoe In Hand

I probably shouldn't admit this publicly, but I like weeding.

(I can hear your groans. I can even sense your eyes rolling as punctuation to the groan. But it's true!)

I like weeding.

Maybe it's because I am a perfectionist, and seeing tidy rows of vegetables and trim perennial beds is almost a necessity for my sense of order. Maybe it's because when my kids were little it was the only quiet retreat available. Maybe it's because I take some kind of sadistic pleasure in causing the death of an enemy.

I just like it, okay?

Almost every day during the growing season I have my hoe in hand and do battle against the ever-present rebellion cropping up, marring my tidy garden plots. And I mean business.

I know many of the beasts by name now. I know where they are most likely to crop up and when. I know a lot of their nasty little habits, and have learned over time how best to fight back.

For example, I learned early on in my gardening career that trimming them off at the top to make the rows look nice for the day does exactly diddly-squat in the long run. I learned that chopping them to bits and leaving them on top of packed soil to dry out does a little better. I learned that the babies are much easier to uproot than the old grizzled grandpas.

Most of all, I have learned that nothing short of a full-scale onslaught will even make a dent in those weeds!

Even before my perennials peek out in the spring I have my hoe at the ready. After the first few warm days, there will be a fresh flush of winter annuals ready to set seed. The rate they grow would be miraculous if it weren't so maddening. And if they set seed early in the season, I know I have lost a huge battle before I've properly begun. Some of those critters can produce thousands of viable seeds each!

I pull the plants out by the roots, pack them in buckets, and haul every leaf off my garden to be burned. And each flush thereafter which gets to the stage of flowering gets the same treatment, all season long.

A bit drastic, you say? With a hint of paranoid-violent?

But this is war . . .

Yes, it is time-consuming. Yes, it gets tiresome when the day is bright and there are many other things calling for my attention. Yes, some days I do it the lazy way and then reap the due penalty later with a fresh flush of odious offspring. But the change in my garden over time has been dramatic!

Where once thousands of tiny seedlings would germinate and form a lush green carpet, it became hundreds, and then tens. They still sneak in on the wind or from a weed my hoe inadvertently missed, but the battle has become an occasional skirmish. Weeding is much more enjoyable when the problem is more or less kept under control with due diligence.

Oh, for the wisdom and foresight to go through my heart's garden, hoe in hand, ready to do battle with everything that is 'weedy' that tries to sneak into my heart!

Think about it. Nasty habits are so much easier to root out when they are just 'babies'. Caught early on, they haven't time to establish a deep, tough root system. Or go to seed and multiply at an ungodly rate while we sit back passively and watch them entwine themselves in our minds and spirits. Sin is best dealt with proactively, with an awareness of how sneaky it can be, watching for the ways and places they are most likely to show up.

But being constantly on the alert—doesn't that get old? Tiresome? Would you rather deal with the little guys or a full-blown invasion?

"Consider Him (Jesus) who endured such opposition
from sinful men, so that you will not grow weary and
lose heart. In your struggle against sin, you have not
yet resisted to the point of shedding your blood."
(Hebrews 12:3-4 NIV)

Yeah. No kidding. How hard have **you** been resisting sin? Most of the time we don't put up any resistance at all, and then wonder why we are crashing and burning so badly!

I take great pride in the condition of my **garden,** and am willing to do what is necessary to keep it in order. How much energy have I expended to keep my **heart** in order?

Lord, make us a people who will do battle diligently in our own hearts for the sake of Your Kingdom! Teach us to stop and consider Your Son, who battled so bravely on our behalf.

Looks like I might need another hoe . . .

True To Type

I am frequently amazed at the infinite variety of plants in the world. Living on the Canadian Prairies limits what I can grow, but there is a dazzling selection nonetheless!

Take lilies for example. They are easily the champions in my July garden. From nodding to down-facing to staring at the sky, these star-shaped blossoms add elegance and refinement to my borders. Buds and blooms alike are regal in their mid-summer glory. Defying all odds, they spring forth from an onion-like bulb year after year, remaining beneath the winter-blasted earth until they can rise in brilliant splendor on stiff sturdy stems.

Or evening-scented stock. Not much to look at but oh! the burst of sweet candy fragrance as the sun goes down! Or monkshoods. Named apparently for each blossom's resemblance to—well, a monk's hood—these stately perennials explode in purple and blue spires later in the season when many other perennials have packed their display away.

And a recent favorite—yellow loosestrife. A sterile cousin to the native plant which is classified as a noxious weed, this gem produces yellow spikes on bushy, copper-leafed plants for most of the summer. Not to mention hens-and-chicks. These are **so** cute! Compact rosettes of pointed stiff leaves produce 'babies' on stolon tips that look ludicrously like what their name implies.

If you are wondering if I am just going to name and describe all of my favorite plants, don't be alarmed. (It would take **way** too long!) But I do want to use the wonderful variety to illustrate something that we all know but often 'forget' during the day-to-day activities of our existence.

We are unique.

(Bet you've heard that one before, haven't you?)

But I mean it. Really, really unique. Like plants, we have different forms. Some of us are stiff and tough. Others, delicate. Still others, gorgeous. Graceful. Regal. Squat. Colorful. Lanky.

We also serve different functions in our homes and workplaces and communities. Some are the backbone structure, like trees and shrubs and fences. Some don't look as fancy but add an incredible fragrance of thoughtful self-sacrifice to everything they do. Some are sweet 'eye-candy'! Others are medicinal, with the gift of spreading vitality and encouragement wherever they go. As varied as the world of botany, each of us serves a purpose and adds to the fabric of daily life in different ways, during different seasons, serving different roles.

So what are **you** adding to the garden?

My garden would not be the same if I removed bits of it. There would be holes, disharmony. The texture and balance would change. The unexpected delight of discovering something growing in its own special spot, tucked in to add its particular fragrance, would be gone.

A garden filled with all one type of plant? Boring. (Yawn).

I have spent a lifetime trying to imitate (or rival) my neighbors. Break dormancy like them. Grow at the same pace as them. Bloom like them.

Produce fruit like them.

How foolish. One of the most important garden truths is this—plants grow **true to type**. In other words, a delphinium always grows like a delphinium. Roses don't suddenly decide to adopt the habits of a cactus. Evening scented stocks don't abandon their scent to join the plain-smelling daisies. If I plant bean seeds, it is a mathematical improbability that carrots will grow in their place.

So what is your role? Who are you, **really**? (Not who you think others **expect** you to be . . .)

> *"There are different kinds of spiritual gifts, but the same Spirit is the source of them all. There are different kinds of service, but we serve the same Lord. God works in different ways, but it is the same God who does the work in all of us."*
> *(I Corinthians 12:4-6)*

Stay true to type. Are you the practical, go-to one? Go for it! Have a creative flair? Create! Understand what's under the hood of a car? Serve your clients with pride. Have a knack for connecting with people? Socialize with intent. Understand that whatever your 'thing' is, God created you with exactly those characteristics because there was a 'you' missing in the world. He has a purpose and plan beyond your imagination—a way of showing off your unique style while blending you into the greater 'Global Garden'. Digest this amazing truth—without your presence, there is a hole, an imbalance, a flaw in the design that mars the magic of magnificence.

Grow true! Take your place with dignity and work conscientiously at being the best you possible, with the knowledge that you matter. Count. Are irreplaceable, in fact.

An integral part of what God wants to build into His Kingdom for His purposes, in His own way and time.

No more copy-catting someone else. We need **you**.

Stay true to type.

Whistle While You Work

I spend hours working in my garden every summer.

I plan. I plant. I weed. Prune. Harvest and eat. Stake, fence, and tie. Remove dead growth. Rake. Scatter seeds, destroy insect pests, powder, spray, and mist.

Water. Fertilize. Repeat. Pinch off spent blossoms. Check and recheck. Twine vines around trellises to train them where I want them to grow. Install flat landscaping rocks. Build pathways. Plant bulbs.

Look for buds. Watch for disease. Prod, pluck, nurture, nudge. Cut back overgrowth along pathways. Watch bees. Add compost. Top up mulch. Redesign perennial beds. Observe growth habits to determine which plants to move where and when. Transplant flowers to new locations to better show them off. Add and remove protective winter cover. Dream. Scheme. Grin encouragement at every new leaf, bud, shoot, stem, flower, tendril of vine, fruit.

Wow. It makes me tired looking at the list, the never-ending work-in-progress list of gardening chores.

Except when I am in the garden, it isn't a chore. It is more an act of expectant love, a brooding and protective hover over my domain, a joy-in-waiting. I usually hum as I go about the tasks of the day in complete contentment, knowing that the overall beauty in the making is worth every effort, every dirty or broken fingernail, every sore back muscle, and every moment of labor.

Often I whistle as I work!

I know very well that the recipients of my dedicated hours are not grateful. They are unaware of my laborious input into their existence. So why keep working on a lonely and unappreciated project?

I guess it's because I can see past the sweat equity to the beauty that is on its way.

My friend, we grow in a magnificent garden, one of the Master's design. He spends hours in it, feeding, watering, and pruning. He watches over it, hoe in hand, searching for pests and weeds and worms. He takes great delight in every new leaf and bud and sign of potential growth. He walks the pathways often, interested in your efforts, delighted at a new root tip, thrilled with every movement upward.

We are often unaware of His presence in the garden. We feel the nip of a pest taking a bite, bend in the wind, break under the weight of snow cover, tingle in the frost, and cry as we stretch tender roots into harsh, compacted, drought-crusted soil. We sense sun, drink rain, and forget that all that is good is from His hand.

In God's garden, all that we see as difficult and painful and grim is monitored moment by moment; these, too, are in His hand, completely under His control. Though not of His design, He is constantly hovering, seeing with wise eyes how they can be incorporated into the overall pattern and composition to create strength, uniqueness, beauty, completion, maturity, more fruit, more bountiful flowers.

Why would He bother with the unending, largely unappreciated gardening tasks? Tying us up after a strong wind? Pruning and trimming and weeding and watching?

Because the Master Gardener, seeing end from beginning, knowing harvest from planting, sees the beauty and sees that "it is good." His heart delights in our development, our every baby step toward maturity.

His heart likewise hates all that holds us back, harms us, destroys what we were created to become. He takes an active interest in helping us to grow strong enough to participate with Him in rising above the disease and pests, storms and drought. He knows that our troubles make us aware of His ever present activity in the garden. Open our hearts to seeing Him as He is. Free us to run to Him with all our might, entering into a complete, genuine, beautifully vulnerable relationship with Him.

There is nothing in the Bible to suggest that God whistles, but I do know this: He sings as He works!

> *"The Lord your God is with you, He is mighty to save.*
> *He will take great delight in you, He will quiet you*
> *with His love, He will rejoice over you with singing."*
> *(Zephaniah 3:17 NIV)*

You are a Love Project in the garden, in the hands of the Most High! Grow, friend!

And don't forget to listen. Your song is crooned over you as the Master Gardener goes about His work in your life. The melody is unique—a personalized lullaby sung by a Father deeply in love with you, His child.

If you hear it today—whistle while He works!

Windstorm

Once in a while terrible things happen.

Windstorms scream in, out of the blue.

Your garden is progressing magnificently. There has been more than adequate rainfall. Sunlight hours have been lavish and abundant. Temperatures have not been in either extreme. Miraculously, insect pests have been at a minimum and you have been able to easily handle the strays. Weeds, too, have been kept at bay.

Everything is going great.

A lovely lull in the battle.

And then a freak windstorm hits.

Wind is actually an integral part of a garden. Wind distributes pollen and seeds. It brings in pests and their predators alike, usually keeping an incredibly taut balance in the cycle of life. It creates the tension that encourages plants to reinforce their structure to withstand it.

It's all good so far, right?

But wind at its worst is just plain nasty. It knocks over towering delphinium spires, a more efficient 'make-work project' than any government could have contrived. It scatters delicate fruit blossoms, with the potential for substantial fruit loss for the year if it comes at the crucial pollination phase. It can knock over rain barrels, garden sculptures, fences.

And it can cost years of growth and development in the blink of an eye.

In my little orchard is a magnificent crab apple tree. Its form used to be perfect. Well balanced and beautifully proportioned, its branches supported a stunning display of fragrant white-tinged-pink blossoms last spring. It was absolutely breathtaking. One of my favorite spring moments was a stroll beneath that scented canopy of white, listening to the bees going about their business, letting the dappled sunlight throw its perfumed flirty shadows across my skin. I would drink in the moment—pure, quiet, and magical.

That tree holds lots of memories. Spread low and wide at the base, sturdy branches have given my children their first climbing triumphs. Alternately a tent or a castle, imagination flourished underneath its fragrant canopy. Boxes of tart, juicy apples were transformed into juice, jelly, and pies.

A windstorm took a third of it in a nanosecond.

One entire side of my lovely tree was snatched away. The perfection of form, the graceful balance, ruined. I shed tears as my husband and son cut those huge broken branches into more manageable chunks and hauled them away, one by one. When they were gone, a further problem was revealed. One large remaining branch was now unwieldy, awkward, out of place.

It had to go.

Ouch. With that branch cut away, I have lost fully half of the tree that I so love, planted so long ago by my husband's grandmother. So many years of growth and fruit and memories . . . gone.

What has the windstorm in your life stolen from **you**?

There comes a point when no matter how well you have worked at maintaining your heart's garden, tragedy strikes. It is unexpected and unwelcome. It's not your fault; you could not have prevented it had you tried. And it leaves in its wake a mangled path

59

of damage that **you** have to clean up. The injustice of it hits you like a sledgehammer.

Now what?

The windstorm takes many forms. Death. Disease. Abuse. Financial ruin. Lay-offs. Natural disaster. Crime. And it robs us of comfort, innocence, peace of mind, stability, sanity, possessions, courage.

And the hope we will need to fight back from the brink of disaster.

I wish I could tell you I had learned the secret of the windstorm. That I have conquered and risen above and triumphed. I haven't, plain and simple. As many days as I stand tall, I am knocked back to my knees by aftershocks that seem to just keep coming. But I can tell you this . . . in the midst of the wind, in the terrifying howl and swirl and mêlée that are so discouraging and so disconcerting and so damaging, I have found moments of impossible peace.

Impossible because when the wind becomes a gale and then a tornado, there is no reasonable explanation for experiencing joy in its midst.

The best place to be is in the eye of the storm, holding the Master Gardener's hand.

*"Peace I leave with you; my peace I give you. I
do not give to you as the world gives. Do not let
your hearts be troubled and do not be afraid."
(John 14:27 NIV)*

The world gives peace only when things are going well—during an 'apple tree stroll'. Jesus promises what we truly need—calm in the crisis, in the moment of trauma, at the door of disaster, when predicaments push us past the breaking point.

So in this storm, I cling to the promises of One who loves me and gave Himself for me and is willing to see this project to its rightful conclusion. When peace comes, I rejoice in triplicate in case the next time I don't quite pick it up. When peace tarries, I wait.

Because one day, my apple tree will be completely restored. (Figuratively, of course.)

Mmmm, it's gonna smell **good** . . .

Anchor Your Arch

I fell in love at first sight . . .

It was Japanese-inspired, stately, unusual.

And on sale, too!

The combination was too good to pass up. I squeezed it into my little car and lugged it to the garden and set to work on the 'some assembly required' part of the transaction. A few grunts of frustration later (who do they get to write these instruction manuals, anyway?) my beautiful garden arch was ready to be planted in its regal new place of honor, framing an existing paving-stone walkway.

I was somewhat perplexed by the flimsy foot-long spikes that were to be attached to its base and driven into the ground. *Will they hold up?* I wondered, unsure.

My husband wasn't unsure in the least.

"That's all that came with it? You're kidding. There's no way those sticks will hold this thing in the ground. The first little wind that comes along is going to blow it right out of the yard," he informed me firmly. Noting my crestfallen features (and the pitiful puppy-dog eye that I have perfected over our 20-year marriage), he added, "You need a deeper anchor." After I sat dejectedly right on the ground in hopeless defeat, he added kindly, "Do you want some help?"

The poor, poor man . . .

Being handy with a welder, he set to work. I thought he might add some heft to the inadequate spikes that had come with the package. Boy, was I off . . . He not only added lengths of solid steel to the four main posts, he welded a solid bar across the bottom of them, effectively building an underground cage.

"This way, the structure will stay square—no twisting in the wind," he explained. "Plus, it's deep, so there's absolutely no way that this thing is ever going to blow over. Ever."

I batted my eyelashes and added the appropriate praises as he helped me carry it across the yard from the welding shop to its final destination.

I removed the paving stones which were in the way and enthusiastically grabbed a shovel, eyeing the lengths of steel to gage the depth I would have to dig. After the first 8 inches of soil were scraped away, I hit solid concrete. (Well, actually, it was heavy clay, but it certainly *felt* like I was feebly chipping away at cement.)

My enthusiasm melted away like a cup of water into parched sawdust.

Hubby, seeing the situation and being the gentleman that he is, silently grabbed another spade and started to dig.

Let me tell you, it was back-breaking, nail-chipping, hand-dirtying, sweat-inducing, grumble-laden work. We strained and dug and measured (and dug) for what felt like an eternity. Finally, my husband said the hole was deep enough. Together, we stood the massive underground cage with its delicate Japanese upper story into that cavernous hole, and replaced the heavy clay mass around its base.

More sweat. More grumbles.

Finally it was time to lay the paving stones and survey the results. By this time, I was so exhausted, I no longer cared whether the dang thing would blow away or whether it was straight and true, or level, or anything else. I just wanted a cool shower and a nap.

Thinking about it now, I smile. I can't tell you how many beautiful vistas I have glimpsed through that archway. How many delights have bloomed alongside it, or winding their way through its beams. How much it has added to my landscape, a delightful balance of structure and purpose and artistic flair. How very straight, level, and resilient it has been through many storms and winds and weather elements that would love nothing else but to see it collapse in a quivering heap.

And I wonder—if I was willing to go to all that trouble in my physical garden, why am I so lazy when it comes to investing in my inner garden? My personal, private sanctuary.

My soul . . .

If I have invested nothing internally to give me strength, endurance, or structural integrity, how can I expect to stay strong in a storm? How can I prevent collapsing in a quivering heap if I have only relied on my own two flimsy legs?

What I need is a solid base of superior steel, designed for longevity, on the level, plumb-line true. And let me tell you, it didn't come with the original package.

I need some help with this one.

"I love you, Lord; you are my strength. The Lord is my rock, my fortress, and my savior; My God is my rock, in whom I find protection. He is my shield, the power that saves me, and my place of safety."
(Psalm 18:1-2)

Do you want to be secure from every storm? Rock-solid in the midst of chaos? Unmovable in the fiercest circumstances?

Invest in your heart's garden. Give it the reinforcement it needs now, in the sunshine, so when the storms strike, you can stand secure, head high, beautiful in stance, poetry in form, a blessing to the eyes of all who behold you.

Do the back-breaking prep work. You'll reap huge dividends from the discipline of daily bible reading and prayer. Dig deep into God's Word. And don't forget to spend time with your Rock and Shield—He has the power to do what you cannot do for yourself.

Anchor your arch . . .

Like A Lily

Ah, the lily.

Nothing in my floral collection has stolen my imagination, captured my attention, or given me more pleasure than these goddesses of the garden, these nymphs of subtlety and grace. I prize my expanding lily collection above any other. I seek out ever more rare varieties, ever broader selections of hues, ever more robust genetics, perusing catalogs and searching on-line for something new to add.

I can't get enough of them.

I love lilies, from the time they first poke their heads out of the ground in spring, showing on their apex their potential bud count for the year. I love the determination of their narrow, stiff leaves which radiate from their single stalk like a shock of green sun-spokes. I love their trim, bushy appearance as they calmly and steadfastly mature in the sun and rain all through May and June. I love them when their buds begin to separate from their top-knot and extend themselves in a race to dazzle the world.

And oh, how I love them when they bloom!

Come July, visitors to my garden are often startled by the number of lilies on display. No two are alike—ranging from pale to spotted to perfumed to vivid to splotched to streaked, their display boasts the triumphs of modern lily breeding and screams the infinite creativity of an infinite God.

I am delighted when each of my new acquisitions blossoms for the first time, and I can see for myself what its personality is. I often stroll among the lilies in the evenings, amazed at their subtleties, enchanted by their glory. I drink in their beauty and scent. I rejoice with them in their triumph and splendor. And my heart resonates in a wild hope with the words of Jesus.

> *"**Look at the lilies of the field and how they grow. They don't work or make their clothing, yet Solomon in all his glory was not dressed as beautifully as they are. And if God cares so wonderfully for wildflowers that are here today and are thrown in the fire tomorrow, He will certainly care for you. Why do you have so little faith?"***
> *(Matthew 6: 28-30)*

Wow.

God Himself 'cares so wonderfully' about these lilies! Their variety and beauty suit His artistic nature, His intrinsic pleasure in anything that dazzles the eye and feeds the soul. And if He can care about such as these, your beauty certainly astounds Him and causes Him to draw His breath in sheer appreciation as He beholds you, His own, His uniquely handcrafted masterpiece, His treasure.

Why do you have so little faith?

Why do I have so little faith?

Why, indeed . . .

If a cement truck backed into my garden and spewed its venomous lime onto my lilies and covered them in a wasteland of impermeable concrete, if a sewage tank ruptured on its fragrant display and caused it to reek to high heaven, there could be no closer image to describe what this evil world system does to those in its grip. A daily diet of grunge and despair over the centuries since Eden has so coated our eyes with a death-film, that we can no longer visualize our worth, our value, let alone our incredible beauty. I see so many of my fellow creatures who have been blinded to their true self.

I see, because I am one of them.

I, too, fight to claim kinship with this impossible fairy-like dream that God plants in my truest self when I read His words. My deepest soul-place cries out to believe, but my eyes in their cloudiness deny the Word's power, snatching it out of my desperate hands in a bitter joust that has become all too familiar . . .

My spirit cries out to become something splendid, to attain what is offered, to appropriate the impossible extended to me.

To be like a lily.

Beautiful. Glorious. Unique and as equally valued as all the other stunning beauties around me. Cared for by the Living God whose hand created them as well as me, in order to express the endless subtleties of His multi-faceted character.

And in eyes of faith the grunge is swallowed, the grave is defeated by One living, the rigid barrier of cement-like casing is lifted by One whose hands were pierced to prove my value. I catch a glimpse of that Love which is so lavish, so astonishing, and so extravagant. The lying cataracts slip and I peek into a world where I am loved and cherished in a way that puts my love for my lilies to shame.

And I know in my core that this is what I have been created for—to seek and love the One whose love sought me first. Just as I know that I will soon forget—the lesson will fall on ears crusted over as I slog through the slime that seeks to swallow me. So I know where I need to stay—in the garden, where the Master Gardener waits for me in the evening, to remind me of what He sees in me. I need to stay in that place. To learn. To grow. To put on the beautiful covering He offers. To shine and bloom in magnificent variations of magnificent colors.

Like a lily . . .

A Predilection For Paths

A garden is not a garden without a path. Or two.
Or twelve.
The more, the merrier, I say. A well-designed pathway can lead your feet to places you didn't know existed. Point you in an entirely new direction as it curves unexpectedly. Beckon your senses to ingest delights you would have missed had you ventured another way.
I am hazarding a guess here that when you tread upon a prettily paved path, you are not thinking of the work that went into it. The sweat spilled over that particular placement of stones. The planning, visualization, and prep work that were devoted to making that site just right for wandering through. You are probably simply enjoying the view, remarking on the surroundings, oblivious to the backbreaking digging, the sore muscles, and the drop-into-bed-exhausted-so-I-can-do-it-all-again-in-the-morning phase of production.

If I hadn't been the one in the planning and executing stages, I wouldn't think of it, either. But since I have been the one to dig and grunt and lift and bend and place and shovel and haul and stoop, I can share a little insight with you.

The area where I put in a new pea-gravel path last year, with my son's help, used to be a weed-infested eyesore, an unsightly plot on the back door of a delicate dream scape. I decided to give it an update. Plant roses. Add landscape rocks. Augment with mulch and manure, creating a corner worth seeing.

After the intensive beautification investment, a path was in order.

My slave—er, son and I dug down along the sides to install lawn edging to properly define the boundaries. We painstakingly scraped the top 3 inches off the rock-hard, impacted path area, depositing this topsoil on the beds around it to add curve and flow to the ground level. We laid out landscaping fabric to suppress weeds, and tethered it in place. We shoveled and leveled the pea gravel. We commiserated with each other over our sore muscles, and took breaks to ease fatigue.

Now, walking over that path, all a visitor sees is the roses. The lilies. The creatively arranged shrubs and rocks and bamboo fencing.

And a tidy length of pea-gravel path, curving at just the right angle to showcase its wares.

Friend, when you walk your life's path, do you grasp the work that went into it?

Do you see the Engineer, walking over the raw site, exclaiming over its potential? Do you perceive the way the Surveyor carefully levels, drains, and slopes the edges so the rain will run off in a storm? Do you sense the Designer choosing just the right materials, suiting your heart's tastes in every particular?

Do you feel the Contractor's muscles strain to the load? Do you hear the grunts of sheer effort as the drops of blood fall, blood shed to ensure your path's course, safety, and heavenly destination?

> *"Trust in the Lord with all your heart; do not*
> *depend on your own understanding.*
> *Seek His will in all you do, and He will*
> *show you which path to take."*
> *(Proverbs 3:5-6)*

You can trust this path, because it was bought with your Savior's blood. He has gone over every square inch of it to test its integrity. He has built in twists and turns that will draw you to unexpected delights which will nourish your soul. He has designed vistas which will give you enough hope to scale even the highest hills.

And—He has purposely left some rough stuff on all sides of it because He knows these things will persuade you to keep to the path. Patches of fog to obscure your view. Thorns and brambles to block your progress when you wander (and you will!). Sometimes there are even strange things which lurk in the dark and terrify you with their eerie groans and wails.

You must not trust your own understanding—you have never traveled this way before, after all. If you are like me, you tend to conveniently 'forget' this little fact. I often catch myself running impulsively through life, assuming that I know more about my journey than God does!

Sigh. How very rude . . .

Your Master Gardener is well acquainted with the terrain; seek Him at every intersection. He is delighted to escort you on the path He has chosen for you, for **your** sake. Humble yourself before His superiority—allow Him to take the lead!

The next time you wander on a garden path, look down. Think of the effort that was laid out before your foot crossed that spot. And remember that your heart's route has also been secured.

Stick to the trail. Walk in confidence.

Your Savior will lead you on the right path.

Humoring A Hydrangea

Hydrangeas are incredibly beautiful shrubs. When I first started gardening, I remember picking up a copy of 'Canadian Gardening' magazine and positively drooling over a bank of vivid blue blossoms from a spectacular yard in British Columbia.

I want to grow those, I thought. I even had a spot picked out in which to plant them.

Then came the day when I realized that we poor prairie gardeners could only dream of hydrangeas in our beds at night—there was **no** way that these glorious gems were hardy enough for my arctic-blasted, cold-cursed, frigidly-frozen back yard.

So I swallowed my sobs, straightened my shoulders, and moved on with my life.

Barely.

Imagine my delight when several years ago plant breeders made huge strides and introduced a new series of 'Prairie Hardy' hydrangeas! Every year there are new and improved varieties to tantalize the serious gardener. This is great news for a cold-climate plant enthusiast.

My only disappointment is that so far, most of the introductions bloom creamy white.

Don't get me wrong, white is all right. Beautiful, in fact; when planted in groups the display of fluffy panicles of purity can be breath-taking. But in my mind's eye, I still picture that bank of B.C. blue.

Now, hydrangeas have a pretty cool secret trait. Many varieties can actually *change* color. Depending on your soil's pH (potential Hydrogen ions), blossoms can be pink or blue, with variations between. If your soil has a low pH and is acidic, then your hydrangeas will be some variety of blue. If your soil has a high pH and is alkaline, your hydrangeas will sport a lovely pink. And the crazy thing is, some seasoned pros actually grow these guys in containers and add lime or sulfur to fiddle with soil pH and change colors back and forth just for the fun of it!

This has some interesting implications for you and me, my friend.

At some point in our lives, our heart's garden soil is going to have some acid hurled at it. An unwelcome addition that throws our schedule and coping mechanisms out of whack. Something sour that radically affects our blossoming function.

Something to turn us blue.

And most of us, in our distinctly humanized way of hiding from pain and flinching away from the nasty, will miss out on something entirely unexpected.

Blue can be so very, very beautiful . . .

The Master Gardener understands, you see, that if He includes a variety of additives in your heart's garden, you will have a chance to grow and stretch and bloom differently than you ever have before. Out of the box, with revolutionary new palette choices. Unique, with incredible variations in shading, texture, and tone quality. And He knows that your new hue will draw out different things in those who are around you, too. Radically inspire newness in the landscape. Point others to His loving arms.

Because nothing is more joyous than to see someone who has been blasted by all that hell's sulfur can muster, turn to the Living

God in utter abandon. Blue in such circumstances takes on a heavenly shade of sheer intoxication and delight.

> *"Dear brothers and sisters, when troubles come*
> *your way, consider it an opportunity for great joy.*
> *For you know that when your faith is tested, your*
> *endurance has a chance to grow. So let it grow,*
> *for when your endurance is fully developed, you*
> *will be perfect and complete, needing nothing."*
> *(James 1:2-4)*

In humoring a hydrangea, the Master Gardener knows exactly what He is doing.

Throw yourself fully into the pH recommendation for you, acidic though it may be. Vibrant color comes at a cost. Perfection isn't achieved without payment.

But rejoice! The testing of your faith brings a rare opportunity, forging the endurance you need to bloom bravely through any circumstance life may throw at you.

With a helping hand, your heart's hydrangea will burst with brilliant blue!

Defeating The Daylily Doom

Daylilies are among my favorite garden guests. They look pretty all season long, even when not in bloom. Their grass-like foliage adds a pleasing texture to my perennial beds. They are virtually pest-free. Like an easy-going friend, their feathers (or leaves) are never ruffled. Unlike most of their cranky neighbors, if I want to move a daylily at any time during the season, I can, and they won't put up any fuss at all. They are simply quiet, contented critters, and for all these reasons, I love them.

And then, they bloom.

It's like the sun coming out after a storm, a smile after a burst of anger, a ray of light on a dark path. The colors are so unique—subtly veined, like a hand-painted heirloom or a baby's delicately translucent skin. Many are ruffled at the edges, frilly as a child's nightgown. The nectaries (flower epicenters) are often streaked a whimsical contrast to the petal shade. Their delights are unending.

Their flowers are not. These beauties are well-named, you see. Daylilies only bloom for just that.

One day.

It's true. Each fragile treasure lasts for *one day*. Each morning means new creation for one, and doom for another. It is like these spectacular creatures are too magnificent to last on a tainted earth; in consequence, they quietly fade on the morrow, ghostlike in their retreat, melting mysteriously into the mist from whence they appeared.

I wonder if it was of daylilies the prophet Isaiah was thinking when He said these words?

> **"Shout that the people are like the grass. Their beauty**
> **fades as quickly as the flowers in a field. The grass**
> **withers and the flowers fade beneath the breath of the**
> **Lord. And so it is with people. The grass withers and the**
> **flowers fade, but the word of our God stands forever."**
> **(Isaiah 40:6b-8)**

It is indeed a sobering thought to contemplate my, our, impermanence. Every TV channel, every magazine, shouts the merits of its anti-aging creams and gray-masking dyes, promising longevity. The whole point of a multi-billion-dollar fitness industry is to cheat death and disease. Diets spring up faster than mutated viruses, promoting products to get the body in tip-top shape, to set back the aging process, to fight the battle of the bulge and provide the human race with more effective tools to beat the demon of growing old into submission.

Now, there is nothing wrong with being in good physical shape. In fact, there is every advantage to be gained. But if we agree with the apostle Paul, aren't we a little unbalanced?

> **"Physical training is good, but training for**
> **godliness is much better, promising benefits**
> **in this life and in the life to come."**
> **(I Timothy 4:8)**

How many advertisements have you seen for products to feed the spirit? How many TV commercials promise benefit to our eternal inner core—the part that will bloom on far after our earthly shelf-life expires?

We are daylilies, friend. Here for a breath in the time line of human history—a mere pinprick on the continuum of forever. It is only God who exists outside of time and space, only His word that outlives hairdos and clothing fads and pop superstars and the 'in' thing of today that is so 'yesterday' by tomorrow. His word never goes out of style. Its truth doesn't change with trends in the political arena or get outclassed by new scientific knowledge, because absolute truth stands the test of time.

Anything worth obtaining is worth expending effort on. Invest your transient daylily beauty with godly permanence. Lean on the words of One who alone can impart everlasting. Grab with both fists God's promises of a life that never ends. Cling to the things that can give you earthly joy—and then outlive this earth's skin and blossom in the dimension to come as well!

Don't doom yourself to only lasting your daylily's day.

Focus on forever!

Maintenance Check

Is a gardener's work ever done?

The grass is cut, the bushes trimmed, the garden weeded, and the compost rotting away merrily. The pots are watered, the bugs squished, the spent blossoms pinched, the shrubs freshly pruned.

You've picked the berries, fertilized the roses, and added mulch to those spots where the cats got a little frisky. Rain barrels are full to the brim. Furniture is in good repair. Trellises stand tall and true.

Paths are tidied, vines are twined, fountains are primed, terraces swept clean. Delphiniums are staked, aphids sprayed, and ungainly branches made 'gainly' once more.

Now what?

With a lull in the battle, this is the perfect time to relax, take it easy, forget the work, and take the day off. Heck, maybe even the entire month. I'm on top of the game, right? No worries. I'll grab me some shade and snooze my cares away.

Er—no, not really.

Now is the perfect time for a maintenance check.

In gardening terms, most troubles spring up after you let down your guard. During vacation. When your back is turned and your eyes are on another prize.

I don't know how they do it, but insect pests seem to have an uncanny sixth sense for an unguarded garden. Weeds wait until you leave them alone for a few days, and then they scream out their marching orders and multiply wickedly overnight, in perfectly orchestrated unison. If there is to be any disease, it will lurk unseen for weeks and explode in full force as soon as you have safely stored the fungicide in the most unreachable, tippiest-top corner of your cabinet, having smugly surmised you are past the danger.

So when the going is good, the good gardeners get going. Out into the garden, I mean, to closely inspect everything, actively seeking the suspicious and deciphering the dangerous, eyes wide open to potential predicaments.

When did you last do a maintenance check in your heart's garden?

> *"Search me, O God, and know my heart; test*
> *me and know my anxious thoughts. Point out*
> *anything in me that offends you, and lead*
> *me along the path of everlasting life."*
> *(Psalm 139:2-24)*

King David understood as he penned those lines that to live the victorious life, marching on paths of God's choosing, he needed a maintenance check. A periodic heart probe, a proactive spiritual analysis of sorts. He knew more than most how disaster stalks in our down-time. How defeat creeps in on the heels of the mundane and secure.

How staying out of the battle can mess with your morality.

Have you come home from vacation, relaxed and cheerful, only to be blind-sided by doubts, fears, failures, and disappointments? Have you noticed how periods of chaos often follow moments on the mountain-top?

Are you trouble-free today? Get out into your heart's garden and perform a maintenance check. Clear the air. Make sure all is well internally, between you and your Master Gardener. It may be that during this lull, there are things He wants you to weed out. Prune. Water. Fertilize. Allow His Holy Spirit the permission He so desires to reach with the light of His presence those places which have been long ignored.

Are you in the midst of the battle? Your Master Gardener may be training you to take your stand against the pests and diseases that rob your joy and kill your witness. He may be pointing out areas and corners that require a steady hand and heart to deal with. His purpose is to bring you to the place where you are willing to allow His control, even if it means you must dig deep and expose painful secrets to His loving gaze.

Either way, don't quit gardening. Don't complacently rest on your laurels while the enemy of your soul scatters weed seeds when your attention is diverted elsewhere.

Fight hard for your heart's garden. It is your responsibility.

Bible—check. Prayer time—check.

Maintenance?

Check.

Fall

"... a time to harvest."
—*Ecclesiastes 3:2*

*"The law of harvest is to reap more than you sow. Sow
an act, and you reap a habit. Sow a habit and you reap
a character. Sow a character and you reap a destiny."*
—*James Allen*

Bitter Roots

In the garden of your heart, as in the vegetable world, you reap what you sow . . .

A number of years ago, a soldierly row of spruce trees stood guard on the east flank of our farmyard. Like their British counterparts which guard the Queen's palace, they were indifferent to the sun, which cheekily shone down in winks, and unruffled by the wind, which whistled and moaned at times in a most alarming manner. Steady and true, they moved not a muscle in their regiment's stance. The years had not faded them. The cascades of time and space had their flints flung back at them by this solemn company.

Then, inexplicably, the southernmost specimen, the largest and most robust of its kind due to its proximity to the end of the row where it had more luxurious elbowroom, faltered. Lost a step. Took on a sickly yellowish hue which was singularly unbecoming to one of its rank and stature.

As the weeks passed, the sallow tint grew more pronounced. Almost imperceptibly, the pallor was handed down the row to the next resident, who hoisted it high and followed in the dangerous path of its brethren. By the time this perverse yellow stain had manifested itself in the third and then fourth spruce, my husband took action.

"Looks like they're all infected. It would be far better to rip them all out and plant a new row, than to watch them slowly die and lose the time we could be putting into new growth," was his pronouncement. I agreed, but oh, what a hole it would make! And living here, where evergreen trees take an entire generation to mature, the blow was deep. Even if we replaced the faithful old regiment with a new planting, I would be a very old woman before their glory neared that of the originals.

The trees came out. I couldn't watch.

Sitting here now, I see some life parallels. I am reminded of a passage in Hebrews.

> *"Look after each other so that none of you fails to receive the grace of God. Watch out that no poisonous root of bitterness grows up to trouble you, corrupting many."*
> *(Hebrews 12:15)*

It makes me wonder what poison was drawn up in that first old tree's roots, that it would go on to steadily infect the entire community . . .

You and I live and grow in community, too. Our roots are necessarily entwined with those of the loved ones around us. How easily one bitter root could dip into a poisonous pond, and infect the whole batch.

How well God understands our function! He gently warns us of poison because He sees how many sources of the nasty stuff are lingering just beneath the surface of our lives.

He knows just how easy it is for us to quench our thirst at that sour source.

Life circumstances had poisoned my water supply—that was not my fault. It happens. But in reacting to the poison, I developed bitter roots. I cleverly hid a rock-bottom self-esteem from those around me—and also from myself. I had built a lifestyle, a habitat of habit, one self-insult at a time, until I reaped poisonous thought patterns, reactions, and behaviors. Strychnine that should have been cut off at ground level was not only tasted, but drunk to the dregs, until it inevitably surfaced in my trunk, branches, and foliage.

God in His compassion noticed every sip. I know it grieved His heart to see His child greedily guzzle formaldehyde when His fresh, pure, bountiful fountain was full to overflowing and well within my reach. He has graciously instigated a path of healing for me which involves uncovering and destroying those roots of bitterness lying deep below the surface.

I haven't enjoyed it. Some days I would rather just go back to the cup of poison because at least it is familiar territory. I would rather leave those painful roots undisturbed than do the heartbreaking work of seeking them out and digging them up.

But I have come to the realization that the battle is fierce, and it is not only my heart's harvest that is at stake. Somehow, since I am connected deeply to my family and community of local believers, it is as much for their benefit as my own that I am well and functioning on as high and lofty a plane as God desires. As a group we are only as healthy as our weakest members . . .

So 'look after each other'. Love deeply. And when you see telltale signals of a bitter root's yellowing, weakening blow, step in. Let God use you to support the walking wounded as they seek to uncover and rectify subsurface damage, freeing them to reap their full spiritual potential.

The only way we will stand strong is together, unified. Roots entwined. Drinking from the sweet Source of all good, scorning the poison ever available to us. Leaning on each other, growing and developing a taste for all that is higher, better, purer, more heavenly.

From bitter, to better, together . . .

Farmers Don't Have A Prayer

I grew up on a farm. I married a farmer. I guess you could say that the rituals of planting and harvesting are pretty much a part of who I am. Tied to my heart-strings. Flowing in a dendritic mass linked to my neurological make-up. Written into my DNA.

You can take a farm girl off the farm, but you can't take the farm out of the girl.

I guess that's why I garden.

And farmer-gardeners watch the weather.

A fraternity of farmers gathered at a coffee shop involves more than idle gossip-mongering in these parts. It can be deadly serious business. From the moment spring arrives, there is speculation. Was there enough snow for sufficient spring run-off? What is the soil moisture like? Will it rain enough—or too much? Will it freeze tonight? When the first tractors take to the open field, it continues. Will the rains come before I finish? Will they come at the right time?

Weather-beaten faces scan the skies for storms and wind and hail and rain all summer, as the addition or subtraction of any of these phenomena can delay growth, boost potential, destroy germination, create conditions ripe for disease, or produce the crop of a lifetime.

All through the fall, the conversations multiply, both in regularity and intensity. Will this dry weather hold? Will I get my canola cut before the frost? Are these rains going to stain and down-grade my barley? How much will my wallet suffer after those Bertha Armyworms ate their fill? Did the weather we received this year allow me to harvest enough top-quality grain to cover my bills?

And in the end, every farmer knows that no matter how much he sweats, or doesn't sweat, curses, frets or stews, he doesn't have a prayer.

He lives one.

I've always called farming a 'Christian' occupation. I haven't seen another like it for the sheer helplessness, the complete and utter reliance on God to give the increase. You see, the farmer can study all the techniques he likes. He can incorporate all the latest products. He can use the most technologically advanced equipment on the market.

And still, he watches the skies. He leaves to 'chance' his multi-million-dollar investment. He takes on odds every year that would cause a seasoned bookie to weep uncontrollably and quiver in the corner.

At the end of the day, no matter what he has or hasn't tried, the fate of his harvest is in the hands of the Master Gardener. After having done all he knows how to do, he waits and folds his hands.

"Jesus also said, 'The Kingdom of God is like a farmer who scatters seed on the ground. Night and day, while he's asleep or awake, the seed sprouts and grows, but he does not understand how it happens. The earth produces the crop on its own. First a leaf blade pushes through, then the heads of wheat are formed, and finally the grain ripens. And as soon as the grain is ready, the farmer comes and harvests it with a sickle, for the harvest has come.'"
(Mark 4:26-29)

My friends, this is how God is at work in the heart-garden within us. The seed is planted. It takes root in the secret underground lair of our deepest soul. It grows and gathers strength.

It freezes. Or suffers drought or is drenched or writhes under the heat of a merciless, blazing sun. And it grows.

It develops blossoms. It is eaten by pests, bowed down by damaging winds, flattened by thunderstorms. It grows on.

The fruit begins to develop. It faces new waves of pests, and is all but shattered by diseases that waft in on the wind. It stains in untimely rains and withers under pressure of encroaching weeds. And still, triumphant, it grows on.

And one day, the harvest is ready—an incredible edible increase that will provide bread to the starving, manna for the masses, oil and pulses and pasta and sticky cinnamon bun treats to feed the world. And it is God who did it, for His purposes, for His glory, to work in and around and through you, pouring out the gift of Himself to a Universe starved for His love.

All you had to do was plant a seed. Prepare your heart-soil for the planting. Open your spirit to His hovering. And in the process, you don't have a prayer.

Live one.

Nasty Nettle Neurosis

You'll soon understand why I nurse a neurosis when it comes to nettles.

Nettles are fairly common in these parts. They like to grow in abandoned barnyards, where the soil is rich and satisfying. They like to hang out with their buddies on the creek bank, flourishing after the spring run-off has slowed to a trickle and there is plenty of moisture remaining for them to feast upon.

Do you get the idea that they are basically lazy brutes?

And that's not the complete catalog of their failings, either. Not even close. I haven't mentioned yet that they are loaded with barbs, hairy bristles which release inflammatory and irritating substances when contacted with skin. First, it stings. Then, tiny red welts like an angry mob of enraged insects creep all over the affected area and drive you mad with their persistent burning. Hanging on to nettles is the definition of disaster.

Not pleasant, let me tell you. My most recent run-in involved some volunteer weeding. I noticed at a Bible Camp I was speaking at that there was an overgrown flowerbed on the premises. And remember—I actually like weeding. So I set to work with vigor.

I quit with increased vigor—mounting on hysteria.

Unbeknownst to me, there was a tiny nettle lying in ambush, likely giggling maniacally. (If only I had been listening . . .) It took many hours to banish the burn.

I learned very early in life that nettles were my personal nemesis. Put to use in an emergency situation, case in point, I learned that they make a horrifying substitute for toilet paper.

Don't try this at home!

Just saying.

Fortunately, nettles are not among my garden regulars. I have found only a few mini-meddlers and made haste to dispatch them with what a passer-by may find slightly over-done vengeance. But I absolutely put my foot down—those monsters are not allowed in my garden plot, thank you very much.

Unfortunately, putting your foot down when irritations and nasty inflammatory situations arise in real life isn't nearly so successful. Sometimes, things happen that are entirely out of your control. The resultant itch and burn and rash and pain take their sweet time to disappear. And it is at this point that we hang on harder, perversely causing ourselves all the more distress.

I'm so glad that my Master Gardener not only knows all about my nettles, He has set a plan in motion to blast them out of the garden!

> *"Where once there were thorns, cypress trees will grow.*
> *Where nettles grew, myrtles will sprout up. These*
> *events will bring great honor to the Lord's name; they*
> *will be an everlasting sign of His power and love."*
> *(Isaiah 55:13)*

Wow.

Neither cypress nor myrtles are native to these parts—they grow in much more temperate areas. I know that cypress trees grace Italian villas with their classically Mediterranean charms. And I found when I did some research that myrtle trees bloom magnificently! The wood is fragrant, and adds flavor to meat cooked over its embers. Its leaves contain the essential oil '*linalool*', which has been proven to lessen stress, improve sleep, and fight cancer. They also contain a phytochemical called '*limonene*', which is used for flavor, as a citrus aroma, and is a natural cleaner and solvent.[1]

So, I make the daily choice to submit my heart's garden to its rightful Master. He has laid plans to remove the sting from the painful welts of injustice and evil I have been smeared with due to my own sins, and the sins of others. If I will let go, He will replace the nettles in my life with myrtle—building an aromatic, beautiful, disease-fighting, stress-busting, rest-enhancing '*objet d'art*'. He is absolutely committed to my process—and His power and love shine through every step of the way!

The crowning touches will only be finalized when I at last stand before His throne in person—but the mystical transformation has already begun in my heart.

Can it get any better than that? Who else would dare promise such a lofty impossibility? Where else can I turn that will give me even a minute portion of this pledge?

Friend, this promise is for your garden, too.

Leave your nasty nettle neurosis in the rubbish heap. Holding on to your hurts is like clutching thorns and nettles—it only hurts you more. Cling instead to the One who alone can take your festering wounds and lovingly trade them, in His time, for myrtle-like magnificence. Allow Him to bestow on you the incredible privilege of bringing great glory to His name—as you trust Him to do a powerful work of redemption in your heart.

Putting Down Roots

There is one garden harvest that is time-consuming to process, but still worth every effort for the reward.

Fresh peas.

Mmmmmm . . . .

I love peas. I love everything about them—I love the way the seeds look, washed out and wrinkled like an elderly gnome. I love the way they swell with moisture when they begin to germinate. I love the way the initial root stalk, in its ghostly white gown, protrudes from the seed coat and wends its way down into the soil.

I love the way the baby plants poke their tentative heads from the earth when they have germinated, with their stiff cloak of tightly entwined leaves. I love the way their tendrils twine as they cling to my pea fence, and the way they bunch together in their neat rows as they get established. I love the way they bloom in soft milky silk, bravely daring a hopeful harvest.

I love it when the pods begin to form at the end of each withered blossom. I love the anticipation as I daily check for pods thick enough to pick and pry open. I love the way the pod sounds as it splits in my search for its tender contents. I love the juiciness of the neat little peas tucked into their green haven. They lie perfectly matched, like—well, exactly like 'peas in a pod'.

And I love eating them. Yum, yum!

This little cycle of life, this curtain-fall of theatrical harvest acted out year after year in my garden, would grind to a complete halt, but for one thing.

Roots.

The first act in this delicious drama has always been roots—for in germinating, the premier page of the script calls for a root. Lowly roots, which will hug the soil, garner the growth, and produce the food that will grace my table—the Grand Finale of productive performance.

Delicious, indeed.

Fruit needs root. It cannot hope to burst forth without it.

When you and I begin to act our play at our physical birth, we need roots. The nurture we receive at the hands of those charged with our care was designed to provide rich soil and germinating opportunity for robust roots to develop. As we grow, we are watered with kisses and encouragement, feel the sunshine of love and discipline, soak up the breezes of companionship and kindness. Scene by scene, we mature, and put out tentative tendrils, and cling to the support of those around us in our upward mobility.

And one day, our lives produce the fruit destined to our credit before the world began.

Our spiritual birth follows the same lines, and uses the same backdrops and theatrical props. We hear God's Truth—as we absorb it by faith, it germinates within our hearts. We begin by putting down
•roots, developing the resources and patterns that will sustain growth and maturity, and give endurance for the journey.

But the soil is God's department in this melodrama. The apostle Paul shared this prayer:

> *"I pray that from His glorious, unlimited resources*
> *He will empower you with inner strength through*
> *His Spirit. Then Christ will make His home in your*
> *hearts as you trust in Him. Your roots will grow*
> *down into God's love and keep you strong."*
> *(Ephesians 3:16-17)*

Where do your roots grow? On what do they depend? Is the soil you draw from enough to anchor you in the days ahead?

No special effects department can keep you growing if your roots are encased in sawdust. No make-up or costume can disguise wilted stems or faulty fruit. No amount of direction on the set can fake fabulous.

> *"And now, just as you accepted Christ Jesus as your*
> *Lord, you must continue to follow Him. Let your roots*
> *grow down into Him, and let your lives be built on Him.*
> *Then your faith will grow strong in the truth you were*
> *taught, and you will overflow with thankfulness."*
> *(Colossians 2:6-7)*

Some of my roots have sought sub-standard soil. It is **my** responsibility to start them in the right direction, to seek the right soil. A proper foundation for building a satisfying life is found 'in Him'—and as both Producer and Director of this show, God delights to build on that foundation. If my roots grow down into His resources, my faith will grow. In this glorious transaction, my heart, encouraged, will overflow with thankfulness—true fruit, a nutritious harvest to myself and all those who perform their roles around me.

So stretch your roots into the secure soil of Jesus' garden. Your performance might not win an Oscar, but the results will sure be delicious!

Mmmmm . . .

Thrown Out

In an inconspicuous corner of my yard, you will find a square cage formed from used wooden pallets. The front section swings open, completing its affinity to said cage. It is within these confines that all my kitchen scraps are tossed. Undignified treatment, to be sure, but for smelly rotten vegetative waste, what more can you expect?

Affectionately termed The Slop Pit, my compost set-up may not be pretty, but it makes up for a lack of curb appeal with its effectiveness. Every year I am richly rewarded with black, crumbly, well-rotted organic fertilizer that my plants pant for.

Or would, could they actually pant.

The trick to compost is to toss in the things you don't want in your house—items such as browning apples. Potato peels. Last night's unfortunate and rather limp salad. Egg shells. That disgusting unidentifiable goop from the bottom of your refrigerator's vegetable drawer.

Now, layer all that with grass clippings, bark shavings, or dry leaves that were rejected by last year's forest in favor of the present year's finery. Add some compost accelerator if you're the impatient type, water it once in a while with your hose, flip the works with an aggressive pitchfork from time to time, and you'll be compensated with a treasure redeeming all that junk you threw away.

Nasty, active little microbes that love the rotten forgotten will have performed their role in the cosmos and created compost, without even being asked. They don't charge a cent for their services, either.

Life sometimes throws **us** on the waste heap. We can feel very abandoned, very betrayed, even by God Himself. Often pain is too deep for words or comfort. In those dark moments, when hope is only a distant dream and happiness a misty memory, it's okay to moan a little. Whimper. Scream. Rage and stomp and mutter.

One Psalmist understood deep pain, and wondered why God had thrown him in the 'slop pit' with all the rotting table scraps. Psalm 102 is the outpouring of a deeply troubled heart. It begins with pitiful, whiny, heart-wrenching words.

And it goes downhill from there.

"I eat ashes for food. My tears run down into my drink because of Your anger and wrath. For You have picked me up and thrown me out. My life passes away as swiftly as the evening shadows. I am withering away like grass."
(Psalm 102:9-11)

Whoa. The writer feels as though God has thrown him on the compost heap, like a rotten hunk of refuse. Like useless grass clippings, withering under the twin trauma of terror and trouble.

Here's a news flash for you—God could handle these olden-day rants, and He can handle yours, too. He is not surprised at any of your thoughts or overwhelmed by your emotions. He loves to hear your honesty. He knows that when you've vented, kicked, fumed, snorted, and sputtered out your anguish—made a stink, if you will—that you'll be calm enough for Him to go to work, turning all that garbage sticking to you into usable material to spur your growth. A funky fertilizer. A mulch material to bring out your latent luster as a living tribute to God's redemptive gift.

By the end of this Psalm, the author has sorted out his angst. The compost has settled and its transforming power is taking root in his heart.

He has not been thrown out. Neither have you. You might just be in that initial smelly phase, when the 'yuck' is firmly stuck to you like a filthy organic fruit-suit.

Give it some time. Allow the sun to heat the mix, the rain to soften the rough bits to mush, and the microbes to eat their way through the nastiest offal, until what remains is a rich, conditioned additive that will create big blooms and fantastic fruit where there was only trash.

No, it won't feel good. Not until some decomposing takes place. It won't be a walk in the park for your nose, either—especially at first.

But you'll wake up one day to discover something beautiful beyond your imagination—and find the smell and the filth are the only things which have been thrown out . . . .

Isn't God good?

Like Autumn Leaves

The world gets swept up in the beauty of the fall season.

There is something so spectacular about shades of crimson, copper, and magenta. Combine pigmentation with plant parts, and you have the makings of a deliciously delightful autumn.

My ash trees exchange their green frocks for fiery yellow. The shade and brilliance of the summer sun, leaves dance and nod to their partners in a formal quadrille, side-stepping and prancing to the beat of an autumn breeze.

The cotoneaster hedge sports incandescent claret; flushed with vintage wine, it blushes and bows as onlookers pass. The mellow green of the various cranberries mellows further until it erupts in a shade of key-lime pie, delectable to behold in its freshly-baked hues.

Tiny, scrappy, straggly shrubs in the natural bush, unnoticed all through the summer, suddenly become bold. Painted gold, chartreuse, burnt-umber and apricot, their spirits rise enough to cavort and caper in their newly acquired finery, easily outshining their more stately and snobbish neighbors.

Each variety of tree and shrub exerts itself to join the parade, dressed in season's best, vying for glory, simpering in splendor.

There is only one problem.

Only the green leaves are alive, you see. The chromatic complexities of the fall festival are but a cover-up, a mask. A caricature of activity, a burlesque of viability, a parody of being.

They are already dead.

Mimicking nature, all people are actors—not just the ones who win Oscars. We play the part to perfection. Our masks in place, our hearts are inaccessible and our outward shell is a thin veneer of virtue, a skin of morality. Our party dresses are so brightly and garishly applied, they become a decoy to the death and decay underneath.

> *"We are all infected and impure with sin. When we display our righteous deeds, they are nothing but filthy rags. Like autumn leaves, we wither and fall, and our sins sweep us away like the wind."*
> *(Isaiah 64:6)*

Isaiah understood that all the ornamentation in the world could not cover our need for a Savior. Like autumn leaves, our rainbow-tinged and superficial efforts can never reclaim the verdant vibrancy of a leaf alive. Without the life-blood of sap in our veins, we are but days from drying and dangling our way to destruction on the crunchy accumulation beneath the tree. From there, decay is inevitable, no matter what superficial spin we put on it.

What to do?

> *"Oh, the joys of those who do not follow the advice of the wicked, or stand around with sinners, or join in with mockers. But they delight in the law of the Lord, meditating on it day and night. They are like trees planted along the riverbank, bearing fruit each season. Their leaves never wither, and they prosper in all they do."*
> *(Psalm 1:1-3)*

To delight in the law of the Lord is to read His words and get to know Him—His likes and dislikes. Meditate on and ingest a steady diet of the Truth, which will help keep our steps from wrong paths. Tarry in His presence, listening and not saying a word. Shed the superficiality of 'playing church'. Obey. Dig deeper and deeper until we grasp how wide, high, and broad His love for us truly is.

Spend time maintaining a healthy tie to the Master Gardener's own heart, establishing a connection to His character, seeking sustenance from His rich supply.

For all their finery, I don't want to be like autumn leaves. I want vitality in abundance, fresh and vivacious and tapped in to the Source of life itself. I want the joy of those whose leaves never wither. I long for my paltry efforts to be infused with the breath of life, producing and multiplying fruit to satisfy not only my own soul, but those around me as well.

Let's leave the falling to the foliage.

Hang in there!

Go green.

Soil Softening

My garden soil is lumpy, bumpy stuff. If it gets worked when it is moist, great clods of fierce fiendish garden goblins surface and dry into heinous hunks of sculpted cement that would make the most gentle greenery enthusiast hurl herself headlong into a garden-rage.

I have actually spent time with a spade venting my frustration in maniacal flailing and hammering tactics which do more for my emotional outlet (and that of any innocent onlookers) than for the soil's modification.

A better alternative is to plant living mulch, a green grove of vegetative matter which mid-season is worked into the soil, amending its stubborn tendencies to clump—slightly. We have tried adding straw and other types of organic matter, various methods of tilling, zero tilling—all with small gains and the inevitable gradual descent into the madness of moronic lumps. I could swear that they multiply in the dark like demented rock-rodents, masses of mortar giddy with triumph.

Good for spade stomping; disastrous for gardening. Trying to sow tiny lettuce or carrot seeds in the midst of such a mess is sheer madness. To hope for a harvest after such dismal seeding conditions is the definition of ridiculous.

Serious soil-swellings may sit for weeks. Spades aside, those lumps are going nowhere fast.

Unless it rains.

There is something almost magical about an army of minuscule raindrops when it comes to breaking up the bumps. What sheer muscles are powerless to accomplish, a gentle rain can do in a quiet combat, a peace-time overthrow of the ridges' relentless rule. The plaster binding particle to particle is broken down without a shot fired, melting molecules whisper-like into a softened state, dispersing and disintegrating the fiercely resistant, mellowing and mollifying, turning rebellious ruin into supple soil, glue into garden glory.

I am not by any means the first gardener to notice this awesome phenomenon. This process is expounded upon in the book of Psalms.

> *"You drench the plowed ground with rain, melting the clods and leveling the ridges. You soften the earth with showers and bless its abundant crops. You crown the year with a bountiful harvest; even the hard pathways overflow with abundance."*
> *(Psalm 65:10-11)*

As the Master Gardener's drops of rain soften the physical earth, His touch can also soften the hardest of hearts. Turn clod to sod. Produce loam from lump. And bring a bountiful harvest from our most difficult circumstances.

Do you truly desire higher? Do you dream of fruitful, bud-laden beauty?

Prepare the soil of your heart.

Jesus expounds upon this theme in His parable about the sower, who scattered seed on a variety of soil types, with widely varying results. His point? Your heart's garden only has potential to bud and bloom when it is permeable enough to allow His truth to settle in, take root, and grow.

And no amount of whaling away at its hard surface with a shovel will amend your heart's soil condition one whit. This is an inside job.

Until you allow God's Word to gently soak in, one raindrop at a time, the stiff surface of your heart will be impervious to seed. The process begins with hearing—I mean heart-hearing, deeply contemplative mental musings that ride the channel to your inmost being. Once the healing rains commence, the seeds can germinate in an ever-softer, ever more receptive garden soil, growing and multiplying until your life can produce food for the spiritually starving—including and beginning with you.

Soil softening. A beautiful, magnificent, pure proceeding to be sure. A holy harvest of righteousness will surely spring from the heart whose soil has been properly prepared.

And take note of whose role is whose. The Master Gardener is the provider, instigator, drencher, and harvest-producer. You are simply the open and ready receiver of the blessings.

Are you prepared to reap richly in those inner spaces where once clods and clumps were the only planting potential?

Let the soil softening begin.

You Gotta Get It All

Tap roots are trouble with a capital 'T'.

Dandelions have tap roots. That means that they have the shape roughly of a carrot—one main long root with little hairy tendrils coming off the sides for good measure.

Tap roots are efficient. They can cover a lot of deep territory with that main trunk. They are strong. Their anchoring potential is almost second to none. They are resilient. When a spot of drought comes they just drive deeper and live off what they have already stored in their underground flesh.

And they are as hard to remove as gum on the seat of your pants . . .

Ever try to pry a dandelion loose? They refuse to budge with terrific tenacity. All that happens is that the entire plant breaks away and gives you a false sense of hope.

False because it only takes a minute portion of that old tap root to remain anchored in the soil, and the darn thing will be back as strong as ever. Actually, *stronger* than ever. I've occasionally seen the rascals multiply and produce two tap roots, evil twins as it were, bent on nothing but producing more of those innocent-looking yellow flower-demons.

And since dandelions are *perennials,* they live for more than one season. Accordingly, even *one* in my garden is a no-no. One will soon become one hundred and then more than you can count. Consuming the precious resources allotted to the choice specimens I have had to buy and care for with so much of my energy, these thieves and their tap roots are Garden Enemy #1.

A variety of eradication procedures can be utilized. There are several effective chemicals which will get right into that root, but chemicals aren't always eco-friendly. Besides, if a tap root is entwined with the roots of a legitimate garden specimen, the risk of spraying is simply too high. Tools resembling wicked screwdrivers are popular, as are cork-screw-like implements marketed for the purpose.

Whatever method you employ, you gotta get it all.

Or it will be back before you can say 'drop dead, dandelion'.

I am just now learning how deeply my heart has been invaded by tap roots. Trouble spots exist that I wasn't aware of, that tiptoed in on some rogue breeze and rooted and blossomed and flourished, with only a passive curiosity on my part. Or I saw them coming and took action, but it was not thorough enough, and a portion of a root remained.

You gotta get it all . . .

If there is fruit in your life that doesn't match your tree, and you have tried unsuccessfully to hack it off, then I'm willing to bet that you have a lingering chunk of tap root lurking deep down in the most hidden core of your heart. And nothing but a radical surgical removal will bring you any relief; dealing with the fruit is way too surface-level.

You gotta go deep for those.

I've struggled on and off for years with bouts of bulimia. To a 'good Christian girl' like me, it was a confusing mess. Where in the world did this come from? I did what I thought I needed to. Buckled up the bootstraps and exerted more will-power. Prayed. Cried. Repented. Was eaten up by guilt. I would chop it out temporarily and it would crop up as soon as I was under stress, like a nasty aggressive salesman.

And I fell. Over and over and over.

I saw the 'fruit' and tried to chop it off my tree, not understanding that it was the tap root I was really after. To get to the root, you gotta go deep.

And you gotta get it all . . .

You literally cannot do this on your own. The damaging tap roots that have so affected your visible growth have grown around wounds that need to be addressed by your Master Gardener in His role as Healer. You cannot outrun them. You cannot will them away. You've got to go deep.

> **"Surely You desire truth in the inner parts; You**
> **teach me wisdom in the inmost place."**
> **(Psalm 51:6 NIV)**

God has taken me to my inmost places because He desires truth. He desires all of me, whole and complete. So by faith, I will participate in His plan to get at those roots, painful as it may be. The overall health and beauty of my heart-garden is at stake.

I surrender, Lord. This time, I leave the tools in Your hands.

You gotta get it all . . .

WINTER

"A time to be quiet . . ."
—Ecclesiastes 3:7

"Everything has its wonders, even darkness
and silence, and I learn, whatever state I
may be in, therein to be content."
—Helen Keller

He's Got You Covered

Winter is the season of waiting.

When Frost sweeps in on his icy chariot, the waiting begins in earnest.

Trees tuck themselves in for a long winter's nap. Perennials slip beneath the soil's surface, retreating to their happy places, nesting in winter's womb until spring should call them out to play. Everything . . . slows . . . down. Completely. Like a hibernating bear, whose heart rate drops to alarming lows, all things botanical turn off the taps and relax into a wintry reverie.

By the time snowflakes descend, they assemble in silence. Voiceless crystals fall onto mute surfaces in a dance of secrecy. Soil and structures alike are blanketed in a monochromatic quilt of frigid purity, a white eclipse, an icy mantle, which sings the garden to sleep.

And while snow sounds the death-knell of the present year's garden growth, it guarantees that of the next.

Snow cover gives some reprieve from both the extreme cold and potentially volatile ups and downs as the mercury reacts to mayhem. Winter here means bone-chilling temperatures and wild thermal fluctuations in any given 24-hour period. The topmost layers of the earth freeze solid. Without sufficient snowfall, my garden is open to onslaught.

No matter how well-equipped and dormant my treasured beauties are, when that thermometer reads forty below zero, their lives are at stake. If they don't receive adequate protection from cold climatic conditions, they simply haven't a hope.

One year, we had incredible November weather. Instead of bundling up in overcoats, we strutted about in shirt-sleeves. I was on cloud nine—until I noticed that my lilacs were starting to put out leaf buds, and spring-flowering shrubs were starting to gear up for 'spring'.

That unseasonably warm spell had disaster following on its heels. A wicked cold snap settled in to stay—and without a protective snowy quilt to snuggle up in after a quick spring-like tease, the botanical world was in for a shocker.

I lost more than a dozen roses that winter. They simply couldn't cope with the hazardous circumstances—when push came to shove, they gave up and went to their reward early. Their drive to survive was seriously undermined by their lack of shelter in the winter wardrobe department.

You and I must also survive and thrive under harsh conditions. Our world has been thrown into chaos it wasn't designed for—family units are breaking down, finances around the globe are precarious, and threats of wars and armed conflicts are on the rise. Political will and private morality lie shattered in mangled heaps at our feet.

At the root of it all is something ugly that slithered into Eden way back when, tarnishing the good that God created and propelling the cosmos into anarchy.

Sin is out there—yes, we can see its unmistakable presence whenever we turn on the news.

And for every finger pointed out, more yet point right back at our own hearts.

**"Oh, what joy for those whose disobedience
is forgiven, whose sin is put out of sight!"
(Psalm 32:1)**

Like a cloak of snow spread over the garden, the merciful love of the Master Gardener blankets our cold hearts with His.

He's got you covered.

This truth is acted out year after year in every snowfall. The wintry curse on all of our garden growth and life is enveloped in a canopy of conservation, a bulwark building a buffer against the frosty denunciation of death and doom. Forgiving power purchased at an extravagant fee insulates our souls from the numbing grip of sin.

We live in a fallen world—but we needn't live fallen!

At times we are already so muddled with the cold that we don't recognize the sheer beauty of it. Our shameful inadequacy is wrapped in so large a bow of grace that we overlook the gesture and can't distinguish the offering behind it. We don't appropriate the present. We miss out on the glorious gift.

Accept God's offer of help and hope. Embrace the protective shield He bestows. In your time of winter slumber, nestle into the cozy calm of the Comforter. Love has provided a way to win over winter!

He's got you covered.

When Bling Beats The Blahs

Winter in this corner of Canada can definitely be 'blah'. Foliage is long gone. Plants with any sense have tucked themselves in for a nice winter nap, retreating comatose far below the snow and ice to wait it all out with stoic fortitude. What remains visible is either pale gray, or dark gray, or—well, a variant on the gray theme. Bits of beige and brown are thrown in to break the monotony. Some grasses boast a light corn-tassel taupe just to show their rebellious spirit, but the trees are locked into a basically boring and pitiful palette.

Until a night's fog paints them in a dream-coat of winter white . . .

Following a humid evening, moisture clings to any and every available surface. If conditions are right, droplets from the air freeze in layers of lacy crystals which become hoar frost. Different than snow, each froth-frost formation clings to its host, and to other molecules, in jaw-dropping arrangements which would put any gallery-inspired display to shame. Feather-light, as the sun beats down in its winter wan, the crystals lose their grip and flutter in fantastic flight paths, arcing and glittering in their descent, only to build new canvases on the snow drifts below, swathing their surfaces in a frothy milkshake capped with whipped topping.

And on some incredible, rare occasions, the hoar frost is jewel-laced, diamond-studded, infused with reflected light, sparkling like no diva on a red carpet in her Academy-award best could ever accomplish. On days like these, even the weeds look winsome in their God-given glitter-gowns.

Nothing can beat that bling . . .

I'll never forget my young daughter's comment on a particularly lovely show of hoar frost. "Mommy, look at all the diamonds! We're rich!"

We're rich indeed.

How often under cold conditions our eyes can't see that the wintry world is draped in diamonds . . . Our vision gets fooled—and winter's harsh dictatorship demands full surrender. Garden growth waves the white flag when he comes to call. Progress in plant life ceases to exist. The botanical world waits with bated breath for the warmth which will spring it from its hibernation prison. As the glory of life gives way to the grim grays of temporary death, the garden settles into blah.

Until God applies the bling.

I watch in wonder the magical transformation when bling beats the blahs, and I am reassured. Because I in my ordinary, in my gray and dull and brown, am slowly but surely being painted in godly fantastic, a uniquely hand-crafted sparkle which radiates from every pore. Heavenly *haute couture*, dazzling in splendor, jewel-bedecked and priceless, in blindingly triumphant white.

And you are, too.

Oh, you and I may not see it every day. We're human, after all! Sometimes the heat of the battle burns the gems away temporarily, and the breeze blows it aside to be crushed at our feet. There may be days and weeks when we are unable to allow the crystals of truth to cling to us; we may reject beautification when our pain sees only its freezing fingers. The length and power of this bitter and frigid season can strip our ability to accept what seems to be a lovely, but wildly improbable, offer.

And the real kicker—it takes a night of fog, of obscurity, of dark uncertainty, to bring out the best glitz and glam.

But if our hearts are free to be affected, nothing can dim the dazzle . . .

> *"I am overwhelmed with joy in the Lord my God! For*
> *He has dressed me with the clothing of salvation*
> *and draped me in a robe of righteousness. I am like a*
> *bridegroom in his wedding suit or a bride with her jewels.*
> *The Sovereign Lord will show His justice to the nations*
> *of the world. His righteousness will be like a garden in*
> *early spring, with plants springing up everywhere."*
> *(Isaiah 61:10-11)*

When the Master Gardener touches a life, ordinary becomes extraordinary. Winter becomes a vibrant spring garden. Blah becomes bling!

Has this lesson sunk in for me? Well, no. Some days I hear the howl of winter and get tricked into forgetting the truth—what God anoints and loves, is beautiful **because** He anoints and loves! But on days when the hoar frost exhibits her extravaganza, I remember—I can cling to the righteousness He robes me with, and allow His sparkle to cling to me.

Go for glamor, friend.

Even during life's winter seasons, you can shine!

The Snow Cycle

Where I live, we experience what I call the 'snow cycle'. The cycle plays out something like this: It snows. We shovel. It snows. We shovel. It snows.

Again with the shovel.

For variation, we throw a few new tricks into the bag. It snows. We scrape the ice off our windshields. It snows. We dig out the shovel—and **then** we shovel.

Or my personal favorite: it snows. We forget the shovel and, shrugging our shoulders with prairie-bred nonchalance and cheerful resignation, we go out to play.

You'll notice a marked absence in the snow cycle. After snow, there is never any mention of gardening. Winter gardening here is like being granted complete tax exemption—a mathematical impossibility.

Instead, I dream of gardening. I add gardening pictures to my Pinterest board. I ogle gardening magazines. I write about gardening on my garden blog. And I wait.

Fully one quarter of my garden's moisture comes from this snow cycle. In an area which receives approximately 400 mm (16 inches) of precipitation each year, farmers and gardeners alike rely on the white fluff to keep the water table healthy and get that season's crops off to a vibrant start. Melting piles of snow are equivalent to dollars in the pockets of my agricultural neighbors. Irrigation is uncommon here, so eyes scan the skies all year in anticipation of water in any form, promising a good harvest down the road.

I resign myself to this snow cycle, with its drips on floors and soak in boots and damp in woolen mittens and salt splash on roads. I endure, with grudging grace, windshield scrapers and frozen breath and vehicle block heaters and numb toes and treacherously icy sidewalks.

And that hateful shovel.

Because I know this: the snow cycle precedes the rain cycle, with its musical cadence of drips and drops. My garden comes to life under its soaking. Soon I can putter in earnest and hang the shovel in the garage where my hoe has been hidden. Before I know it, 'spring has sprung and the grass has riz'. Life in all its forms flourishes under the precious precipitation that was a necessary prequel to radiantly renewed vegetation.

> *"The rain and snow come down from the heavens*
> *and stay on the ground to water the earth.*
> *They cause the grain to grow, producing seed*
> *for the farmer and bread for the hungry."*
> *(Isaiah 55:10)*

So contrary to the opinion of shovelers around the globe, the snow cycle is a blessing. Its temporary minor inconveniences mean long-term gain to the entire world.

As an added bonus, consider the muscles gained in the action. Ponder the opportunity to breathe the fresh air and enjoy the outdoors. Think of the qualities like discipline, good work ethic, endurance, patience which are being built into your character as you ply that shovel.

I know, I know—those benefits appear anemic at best as you flail away on a bitterly cold morning. Those distinctly uncomfortable sensations of snow swirling down your back and frost sneaking up your nose blind you to the glory of the moment, don't they?

Isaiah has a spiritual application waiting for us in the very next verse.

> *"It is the same with my Word. I send it out, and it*
> *always produces fruit. It will accomplish all I want*
> *it to, and it will prosper everywhere I send it."*
> *(Isaiah 55:11)*

Maybe you thought seeding God's Word would be like a walk in a park, or a stroll in a beautiful garden with a million-dollar view. You envisioned reaching out to grab huge clusters of hanging grapes, and imagined cheers as you deposited them into a waiting wagon. Until the snow started falling, and the wind picked up, and it felt like you were sucked into a blizzard, and the garden disappeared under a blanket of impenetrable white.

And you were left holding the shovel.

Sometimes serving is tough. You don't always glimpse growth. It might feel like one burdensome shovel session after another. All you can see is the inconvenience. The discomfort. The disappointment and apparent futility of all your efforts.

Don't give up! If you sprinkle seeds of truth even in a snowstorm, God has your back. Nothing done in His name is ever a waste. He gave His word!

Besides—that spiritual snow cycle is building into you the traits that will make you much more like your Master. Patience. Endurance. Perseverance. Discipline. It is, in fact, a blessing cloaked in an unlikely outline—unexpected training for the glory to come.

And one day, you will wake up to spring—and there will be your garden, soil prepared for planting, sun warming its surface, a vista of green and vibrant and magnificent wherever your footsteps fall.

So submit to the snow cycle.

It always produces fruit.

Smelling The Roses

Winter is a great time to reflect upon this season of quiet obscurity—a time to ponder the deeper, greener lessons of life. I remember reading years ago in a gardening book of the importance of adding a garden bench to your gardening space, or all you'll do out there is—well, garden.

Great advice. Especially to a perfectionist like me.

When I first installed a seating area in my garden, I would sit and enjoy the view—for about a minute and a half. Each time, from that reclined vantage point, I would see the nasty tendrils of a weed taunting me through a neatly clipped hedge, or a rebellious branch crossing in front of a struggling blossom, or a rock out of place in the pathway. It would bug me so much, I would get up and take care of it. And once over there taking care of that particular issue, I would inevitably spy more things to take my attention and 'fix', until it was too dark to see and the gardening day was over. I would head inside, mourning how little time I had to sit and enjoy my new garden bench, vowing that the next day would be different.

It wasn't.

Have you ever noticed how there is always one more task to be completed, no matter how many you have already crammed into an over-padded schedule?

Right. So it's not just me.

When all the time-saving gadgets of the '50's and '60's were being mass-produced, experts were predicting that we would gain hours and hours of leisure, retiring on a ludicrously early time line and enjoying smelling the proverbial roses while our appliances did all the heavy work.

How foolish. Which of those experts forgot to factor in our tendency to overdo everything?

I often hear those around me wishing there were more hours in the day. What would you do with more hours in your day?

Work more?

Some of my life circumstances have forced me to take a break, forced me to my proverbial garden bench. And I am slowly learning that sitting on a garden bench is not lazy, or unproductive, or wasteful. Not if I smell the roses! I mean, really drink them in. Watch how the bees ramble over the petals. Contemplate riveting ripples as the breeze catches their outer edges. Breathe in their spicy, intoxicating scent on a still, hot day. See with the eyes of my heart in order to build up its storehouses for whatever lies ahead.

I now have 5 seating areas scattered around my yard. I use all of them in succession as often as I can. Sometimes I have to physically pick up the bench and turn it at a new angle if I see too many jobs in one direction, so that I will learn to focus momentarily on the beautiful, not the to-do list.

Yes, those other jobs will get finished eventually. But if I don't take time to rest my heart, they will suck me in to a state of obligation that will rob me of the joy of a job well done. Even Jesus left the demands of His to-do list once in a while, escaping alone or with a few of His friends to recharge after a particularly busy day. If the God of the Universe needed a rest for His heart in His human form, who am I to push myself until I break?

*"Come to me, all you who are weary and carry heavy
burdens, and I will give you rest. Take my yoke upon
you. Let me teach you, because I am humble and
gentle at heart, and you will find rest for your souls."*
(Matthew 11:28-29)

Jesus needs to teach us to rest, because He knows we don't truly know how! His gentle invitation is balm to the spirit in a world that whirls to the wristwatch.

Hence spiritual winter, my friend. We need the 'down time' which a season of waiting brings . . .

What will feed your soul this day? Do it! During winter, in the bitter cold, smelling real live roses may not be an option. A nap on a garden bench won't quite do . . . but study ways in which you can rest your heart in any season. I am slowly learning to seek out little things each day that will build mine up and refresh it enough so that the other tasks of the day won't silently suck me dry.

Perhaps a bubble bath is in order.

Rose-scented will do.

Love Me Tender

There is one delicious sign of spring in particular that I am waiting for during this winter weather—the revival of my asparagus patch!

Last year's growth, well over six feet tall, has been left intact to catch snow. As winter winds drive snow in any and every direction, the spindly spires provide a haven, a place for flustered flakes to plow up against. The melted moisture these snow banks represent will set a high, healthy growth potential for the patch.

One of my first gardening tasks after winter wends its way to the Arctic is to cut the now useless woody stalks back to ground level. There is a two-fold purpose—one, removal of overgrowth allows the spring sunshine direct access to the patch, stimulating fresh new asparagus spears. Two, without that heavy jungle of brown stalks I can spot any growth tips easily. Harvest is much easier when I don't have to 'beat around the bush'!

While other perennials are still shaking off their winter slumber and trees are lethargically stirring, asparagus is hard at work. One of the very first to stick their necks above the soil level, tender young shoots brave the chill and begin to take a look around. As soon as the first few appear, I know I must check every morning. Asparagus season is short and sweet. Once begun, it sprints to the finish, so if I want to cash in on the action, I have to diligently pick while the spears are young and tender.

When asparagus tips are just a few inches out of the ground, they are incredibly tasty. I often crunch a few raw as I pick. They taste just like fresh peas, without the shelling hassle. They snap effortlessly and drip with juice.

Mmmmmm . . . . delectable. A succulent gourmet paradise.

If I leave the tips to age for a few more days, they tower tall. A few days more and the nice neat cap of tightly wrapped leaves begins to break open and elongate. Leaf buds separate along the stem, which becomes stringy. As the stalk lengthens, leaves spring out, a stiff, tough mass of globules. Texture changes—now developing an inflexible outer skin, the combination of leaf chunks and snarly outer shell is unappetizing.

Very soon, the stalk is completely inedible.

What a waste of a tender young delicacy . . .

You know, you and I are an awful lot like asparagus spears.

We start life with enthusiasm. We learn early to trust implicitly. We throw ourselves into the enjoyment of the moment. Our hearts are tender and soft in our youth. We have the capacity of a great, deep, tenacious love, and we give it so willingly and freely, like a song.

We get tough so fast! We begin with a stiff upper lip—emotions, after all, are childish. We quickly learn that life is not always kind, so we build a strong exterior barrier to survive. We become jaded. Calloused. Find believing in anything to be too much of a stretch—too much like a leap of faith. We question everything—and not in healthy or productive ways. The learning curve in the school of hard knocks cultivates inflexibility of temper and unyielding dispositions.

Our tender becomes tough.

I wonder why *three* writers of the Gospels chose to record the story of Jesus with the children? His disciples, those partakers of jaded and disillusioned, almost missed it. They wanted to turn away these pesky children who were swamping Jesus' busy schedule. And Jesus made a point of telling His closest friends very clearly,

> *"Let the children come to me. Don't stop them! For the*
> *Kingdom of God belongs to those who are like these*
> *children. I tell you the truth, anyone who doesn't receive*
> *the Kingdom of God like a child will never enter it."*
> *(Luke 18:16-17 NIV; also see Matthew 19 and Mark 10)*

Like a child . . . trusting completely, in innocence. Believing implicitly, from the depths of a pure soul. Accepting simply. Loving in wild abandon, out of a heart fresh and tender in its youth.

Has your heart lost its pliability? Is it past its 'best before' date?

The Bible has some great advice to address that.

> *"Get rid of all bitterness, rage, harsh words, and*
> *slander, as well as all types of evil behavior. Instead,*
> *be kind to one another, tender-hearted, forgiving one*
> *another, just as God through Christ has forgiven you."*
> *(Ephesians 4:31-32)*

Tender. Young and free, like a child. Or a juicy young asparagus tip.

Use this season of quiet waiting to turn back the toughening hands of time. Cultivate a child-like trust in your Master Gardner. Allow kindness and forgiveness to soften you, keeping you sensitive to the Holy Spirit's leading.

Jesus loves me tender.

What a delicious world it could be . . .

What A Sap

Good things come to those who wait.

Winter is wonderful when she comes, but like your crazy relatives, she outstays her welcome. Toward spring, we are all glad to see her backside—and we don't mind if the door hits her on the way out, either!

As snow steals furtively away in its shame-faced retreat, the ground revives. Kissed intimately by the strengthening sun, it begins to absorb and then reflect its caresses. Frost, forced to an undignified surrender, sulks and returns its hydration to the earth in reluctant stammers.

Thus emboldened, the soil soaks in sunshine. Grass, the first to arise after its winter sleep, pulls on a cloak of vivid green overnight. Almost immediately, neighbors greet one another with grins of mischief. Steps are lighter and more buoyant on the streets. The green infects all of us with its breath of hope and renewal. It lights our eyes and you can almost *taste* the spring in all of us. We dance at our chores and our regular tasks are made irregular, baptized by the scent of life-blood in the air.

As soon as the green appears, I look to the trees. I know that they are the next guests at the party! I scan their naked arms restlessly, watching, waiting, impatient for the first signs that the sap is fluid, alive, on the move. On every walk, on every drive, my eyes are roving, straining to catch the very first fog of pale green that will announce their revival. I know in my heart that deep within woody cortex, sap stirs.

I just can't see it yet.

Then comes the day that I convince myself that it is there—the slightest, palest haze imaginable. If I squint, the barely-discernible hue is gone like a mist, a merciless mirage. *No,* I think. *Not yet.*

And when I wake the next day, the green is full-grown. The trees are gowned in the brightest shade of leaf, resplendent in their costume jewelry. Bushes and copses that were bare and thin only yesterday are plump and fertile in their impenetrable cloaks.

I know the sap is gushing with gusto because I can see the results before my very eyes. What was a tentative, whispered hope has become a full-blown reality. I drink it in. My eyes sparkle and I laugh aloud in the mysterious magic of a day that never grows old, even with its annual repeating.

There is a verse in Psalms that has been translated three different ways. **"The trees of the Lord are well-watered . . ." (Psalm 104:16 NIV)** Lovely thought. **"The trees of the Lord are well-cared for . . ." (Psalm 104:16 NLT)** Even better—a more personal touch, that. **"The trees of the Lord are full of sap . . ." (Psalm 104:16 NKJ)**

Now we are getting somewhere.

Everything God has created in the botanical world has a spiritual equivalent. And watching the awakening of a tree in the spring is hallowed ground, my friend, because it so closely resembles His work in you and me. He has designed a tree to receive its life-blood in this liquid vintage of vitamins, this sticky-sweet sap that flows in bark-lined trunks, to teach us that we have a life-sap at our disposal, too.

What a sap it is . . .

You and I have a physical body. It is like a bare tree—the structure is there, but not the life. The potential, but not the vibrancy. The form, but not the function. Until sap stirs in the veins, it remains 'less than'. Beneath its glory. Untapped and under-developed.

Unless the spirit within is stirred by the Spirit of God, true spiritual life is absent.

The Holy Spirit has been sent to our global 'forest' as its sap, the river of life within. His rejuvenating presence supplies the potency that will cover our rudimentary nakedness in His glory, breathing vitality and purpose into our empty and bleak.

> *"The Lord will guide you continually, giving you water*
> *when you are dry and restoring your strength. You will be*
> *like a well-watered garden, like an ever-flowing spring."*
> *(Isaiah 58:11)*

Often in pain His work seems far off. I strain to see His life-breath hovering, and cannot. My eyes scan for green and come back empty.

But I know by faith that as the trees are touched by an invisible sap-stir, so my life is touched by the very hand of God. My Master Gardener has a vested interest in how I grow and develop. He is in the business of recovery, restoration, renewal.

Take heart! God is at work, whether you can see His activity or not. The sap **will** run once again, viscous and true. Growth spurred by this profoundly personalized refreshment will be a delight to all who behold it—a sure beacon in a dark world, reviving the soul like an ever-flowing spring in a well-watered garden.

What a sap . . .

Living By Faith

We got more than 10 inches of snow on Easter weekend this year.

The poor Easter Bunny got snowed in . . .

Mature disjointed pine branches dotted my yard like hideous caricatures of wax figures—frozen in sinister immobility, casting grotesque shadows on mounds of snow, they mocked the calendar, cackling obscenities under their breath. Blown to the earth under the sheer weight of a sopping snow burden, these dismembered limbs stood guard over my sidewalk to terrorize those struggling through the drifts to gain access to my front door.

A few days prior, I pruned my fruit trees in a T-shirt misted with perspiration under the stimulus of a springtime sun. After the snowstorm, I needed sunglasses—that glare of white was enough to make a gal snow-blind.

Trampled, my gardening soul struggled to rise within my chest, struggled to remind me that spring was on its way. But what my eyes perceived pounded a cerebral funeral dirge. The evidence mounted, overwhelming in its insistence.

All five senses screamed Christmas—only my heart knew it was Easter.

What do you do when your senses are so much at odds with your heart?

You live by faith . . .

> *"Now faith is being sure of what we hope for*
> *and certain of what we do not see."*
> *(Hebrews 11:1 NIV)*

That weekend is weaving an insistent object lesson. The unwanted disturbance in my yard demonstrated, in a spiritual microcosm, what faith really is—and how it functions.

Life is so much like a wicked late-season snowstorm. You are on your merry way, making great progress, when something happens—something which causes a great deal of inconvenience. Something which kills your heart's optimism and stashes it in a frigid icebox. Something which tells every sense that it is ridiculous to dream, fool-hardy to desire, impossible to hope for anything but more pain, misery, and devastation.

At times like these, our sensory intake screams winter—even when spring is just around the corner.

Under duress, against all odds, the eyes of faith must see through the circumstances, penetrate the snow banks. With infallible x-ray vision, staunchly faithful perception dares to peel the skin of decay away just for a moment, just enough to glimpse the lively flesh of beauty and promise hidden like a stash of Easter chocolate beneath appalling drifts of snow.

It is these visionary qualities that the heroes of the Bible are commended for—think of Noah, Joseph, Daniel, Moses, Hannah and Paul. Each dared to believe what God said in spite of prison, lions, mockery, infertility, persecution. All became a living, breathing testimony to God's faithfulness for generations of believers to come because of their ability to see past their problems with a flourishing faith!

Living by faith is reaching for spring when it looks like winter. Living by faith is looking past obstacles to the true treasure buried beneath difficult circumstances. Living by faith is allowing your heart to rise up and conquer your nay-saying brain on the strength of God's promises. Living by faith is trudging through the pain and terror of Good Friday—because you know that Sunday is a-coming!

Just as my gardener's heart wisely holds onto green dreams when a glaring white blanket on the ground sneers and taunts, so my inmost self is learning to cling to the Risen One when circumstances are so stacked that my brain surrenders. Screams at me to give up. Points an accusing finger at the snowy evidence and insults me for daring to hope.

My trials are teaching me that I can be **sure** of what I hope for. I can be **certain** of what I do not see. I can trust with the implicit confidence of an infant in loving arms that this Savior, this Triumphant Champion of the empty tomb, is working even now to thaw my wounded heart and banish the frozen wasteland of shriveled dreams forever.

What about you, friend? Do you look around and see only winter white?

Take God at His Word—He walks with you and will never leave you, so lift your faith-shield high! Place your confidence in Jesus, who has conquered sin and death! Learn to look beyond your struggles to the pierced hands and feet of One who loves you enough to give up everything—**voluntarily**—to suffer in your place.

This is tough stuff. This is where the rubber meets the road. 'Playing church' and acting the part won't cut it when the stakes are this high. When your heart's survival is on the line, where will you turn?

Do you have what it takes to see past all that snow?

This is what living by faith is all about . . .

Waiting For Spring

Toward the end of winter, I wait feverishly for spring.

I sense my garden waiting, too. Longing to throw off its unwelcome winter host. Dreaming of supple and elastic, verdant and alive. Panting for the sun's power. Imagining a world awake and industrious once more.

It all began so many months ago. Winter's approach, with warning drumbeat of early fall frosts, rapped a death march for tender annuals, marking their passage to the afterlife. Vegetables and flowers alike succumbed to the suddenly lowered temperatures. They perished, or languished for a few more sunny days only to fall victim to a successive frost.

Slowly but surely, the average nighttime temperature fell below the freezing mark. Daytime temperatures followed. To add insult to injury, day length dwindled, as if signing a treaty to plunge the world into dark barrenness. The very soil itself stiffened into a frozen mass, arrested in its frosty stupor.

For months, the garden has slept the sleep of death.

I have a tendency to deny the wintry world's realities and curl up indoors for the duration. Waiting for spring as I do, winter simply gets in the way of living. But I went for a drive one morning to run some errands and my eyes were open, I mean really open, and I saw. (How often do I just steel myself for winter and not really see?) I put away my groceries, reached for my camera and poured out into the sunshine, eyes peeled, hope aroused.

Rarely have I seen hoarfrost as thickly laced onto trees, blades of stubborn grass, shrubs, weeds—**everything** was blanketed in a glorious delicately crafted layer of frost. I snapped and snapped, trying to capture the unlikely miracle of beauty in the midst of a weary wasteland of cold and ice, and I knew.

My heart can learn a lesson here . . .

I have been the garden, frozen into enforced immobility, pain crusting my eyes shut in a dark and dreary wilderness of comatose misery. And in the dark, in the snowstorm, in the limited visibility of a raging wind, in my rebellious desire to write my story differently, I have forgotten.

Even in winter, purpose prospers. Enforced down-time is not a waste. My garden needs a slumber period, a time to recharge. The trees and perennials are designed for it. Above ground, while temperatures plummet and snow shrouds the earth's surface, the roots and bulbs lying beneath are patiently awaiting the day they know is coming. They will once again stretch their heads and peek out without risking injury from the cold conditions; they will drink in rain and breathe wind and charge their batteries on the power of the sun.

And yes, spiritual winter is painful. We wouldn't choose it. But even in the dark, under a heavy gray sky, there is beauty if we will open our eyes to its true nature. Seeing it, the spark that is truly **me** is pumping strong in my chest, learning to live with winter's realities while waiting for the promise of spring. Watching as the days begin their gradual ascent into the longer, warmer, greener that **will** come, I learn that I can live today—now—knowing that the best is always yet to come.

Hopeful, I allow my God to train my eyes to see. I start the retraining process of discovering beauty in broken and frozen places. I begin basking in the warm glow of His thawing presence, and feel the stirrings of something truly alive unfolding in my very core.

As the cycle of seasons, so the cycle of life. It ebbs and flows, freezes and thaws, tears down and builds up. Each season has its place in the cycle. Each wintry experience we wade through has potential to build into us resilience, character, and a spark of true Life.

If we let it.

In the words of Jesus, "***The thief's purpose is to steal, and kill, and destroy. My purpose is to give them a rich and satisfying life."*** *(John 10:10)* Some translations label it as 'abundant life.'

In the middle of an emotional winter?

Yes.

When the spiritual wind-chill is dangerous enough to freeze exposed skin in minutes? When the thief of a driving snowstorm obliterates all but the pain?

Yes and yes!

I cannot tell you that I have found the secret to this abundant life. Not truly, not yet. I can tell you that I have experienced just enough joy in my treasure hunt to be convinced of its existence! Along with you, I seek **more** of this Jesus who has the audacity to promise **life** in the midst of a harsh winter!

And I wait. As do you, friend.

Quietly. Expectantly.

Because winter is not a waste. And **spring** may be just around the corner . . .

ENDNOTES

^{1.}   I found my information about myrtles on these websites: 'Encyclopedia of Spices', at www.theepicentre.com, and 'Organic Facts', at www.organicfoods.net.

CPSIA information can be obtained at www.ICGtesting.com
Printed in the USA
LVOW051923060912

297713LV00001B/46/P